LESSON STUDY

STEP by STEP

*How
Teacher Learning Communities
Improve Instruction*

Catherine C. Lewis and Jacqueline Hurd

HEINEMANN
Portsmouth, NH

Heinemann
361 Hanover Street
Portsmouth, NH 03801–3912
www.heinemann.com

Offices and agents throughout the world

The authors and publisher wish to thank those who have generously given permission to reprint borrowed material:

"A Closer Look: The Role of Outside Specialists in Japanese Lesson Study" by Tad Watanabe from *Lesson Study: A Handbook of Teacher-Led Instructional Change* by Catherine Lewis. Copyright © 2002. Published by Research for Better Schools. Reprinted by permission of the author.

"A Closer Look: Why Reteach Lessons?" and "A Closer Look: Blackboard Use" by Makoto Yoshida from *Lesson Study: A Handbook of Teacher-Led Instructional Change* by Catherine Lewis. Copyright © 2002. Published by Research for Better Schools. Reprinted by permission of the author.

"A Closer Look: Lessons from the History Classroom" by Matt Karlsen and Peter Thacker from *Lesson Study: A Handbook of Teacher-Led Instructional Change* by Catherine Lewis. Copyright © 2002. Published by Research for Better Schools. Reprinted by permission of the author.

Figure 1–1 and excerpts from "Contrasting Views of Professional Development: Traditional vs. Lesson Study" by Dr. Lynn Liptak from *Lesson Study: A Handbook of Teacher-Led Instructional Change* by Catherine Lewis. Copyright © 2002. Published by Research for Better Schools. Reprinted by permission of the author.

Library of Congress Cataloging-in-Publication Data
Lewis, Catherine C.
    Lesson study step by step : how teacher learning communities improve instruction / Catherine C. Lewis and Jacqueline Hurd.
        p.   cm.
    Includes bibliographical references.
    ISBN-13: 978-0-325-00964-3
    ISBN-10: 0-325-00964-3
    1. Lesson planning—Study and teaching.   2. Professional learning communities.   I. Hurd, Jacqueline.   II. Title.
    LB1027.4.L49   2011
    371.3028—dc22   2011001315

Editor: Victoria Merecki and Katherine Bryant
Production editor: Sonja S. Chapman
Typesetter: Cape Cod Compositors, Inc.
Cover and interior designs: Catherine Arakelian
DVD tech developer: Sherry Day
Manufacturing: Steve Bernier

Printed in the United States of America on acid-free paper

15   14   13   12   VP   3   4   5

Contents

Preface

In the last decade, the Japanese practice of lesson study has been embraced by teachers around the world. In North America, we now have examples of lesson study in a wide variety of subject areas—mathematics, language arts, history, and so forth—and from the pre-elementary through university level. A number of lesson study efforts in North America are now a decade old, and evidence is beginning to accumulate that lesson study can improve both teachers' and students' learning (Lewis and Perry 2009/2010; Perry and Lewis 2010). The robust communities of lesson study practitioners emerging around the world reveal that many educators outside Japan are eager for a practical means to investigate and improve instruction and to accumulate and spread knowledge about teaching. Lesson study is a tool perfectly suited to enact the "professional learning communities" and "schools as learning organizations" called for in recent North American reforms. Yet lesson study continues to represent a paradigm shift for most educators outside Japan. This book is designed to support new groups who want to begin the journey of lesson study and also to help experienced groups who want to deepen and spread their work.

So How Did We Each Get Interested in Lesson Study?

From Catherine

I became interested in lesson study in 1993, while sitting in Japanese elementary classrooms finishing up a study of Japanese elementary school life (Lewis 1995). I found myself learning much science, though it had nothing to do with my initial research focus. Captivated by students' hands-on experiments and their vigorous debates about physical science, I suddenly began to notice levers and pendulums everywhere in the world around me—can openers, swing sets, my long-handled suitcase. Presumably those levers and pendulums had been there all along, but something about the Japanese classroom lessons led me to suddenly notice them. I asked Japanese elementary teachers how they learned to teach in a way that sparked so much thinking about the physics in daily life. Japanese elementary teachers, like their counterparts in many other countries, are generalists who teach all subjects. To my astonishment, Japanese teachers told me their teaching techniques had come in large part from the United States. Public "research lessons" allowed these new science teaching strategies to spread more easily across Japan than across the United States. Research lessons—lessons specially planned to collaboratively investigate some aspect of teaching—are a central feature of lesson study, allowing Japanese educators to examine and accumulate knowledge about teaching. As a researcher who speaks and reads Japanese, I have observed lesson study and interviewed lesson study practitioners in Japan since 1993 and in the United States and other countries since 1999.

From Jackie

I became interested in lesson study in 1999, while serving as an elementary teacher and half-time mathematics coach at Highlands Elementary School in the San Mateo-Foster City School District (California). With colleague Mary Pat O'Connell, I was looking for a professional development model that would go beyond "pushed-in" or "top-down" approaches and would support *teachers* to lead sustained improvement of classroom instruction. After reading about lesson study in *The Teaching Gap*, I felt certain I wanted to do lesson study. How to do it was much less clear! Mary Pat O'Connell and I began by recruiting two other local math coaches, Barbara Scott and April Cherrington. We wrote an open letter to teachers in our district, and recruited twenty-seven volunteers who were interested in trying out lesson study. Since 2000, our work in San Mateo-Foster City School District has grown steadily. Although Mary Pat O'Connell and I have both moved on to another district where we each have new lesson study colleagues, lesson study continues at both Highlands School and in other settings within the district. Highlands' efforts have also helped spread lesson study around the Bay Area.

Recently, in Chicago, we met a group of young teachers who had just finished their first lesson study cycle. They had difficulty containing their excitement about what they had learned about mathematics and student learning from their work together. They clearly felt empowered to improve instruction, supported by their team, and connected with colleagues (in their district and at a nearby university) who would help them continue to deepen their knowledge. The team shared topics they looked forward to investigating in their next lesson study cycle. They brought to the hard work of instructional improvement traits that we see over and over again as we meet colleagues involved in lesson study—a fascination with the puzzles of subject matter and its teaching, a deep curiosity about student thinking, an urgent sense of responsibility to improve instruction, and the willingness to have hard conversations. At a time when so many educational policies fail to recognize and nurture the capacity of teachers to improve instruction, we feel enormously grateful for the learning community lesson study has brought to us. We hope this handbook honors and in some way deepens the work of our many lesson study colleagues and brings more teachers into the lesson study community.

Acknowledgments

This material is based in part upon research supported by the National Science Foundation under grants 9814967, 0207259 and 9355857. Any opinions, findings, and conclusions or recommendations expressed in this publication are those of the authors and do not necessarily reflect the views of the National Science Foundation. The Kabcenell Foundation, Noyce Foundation, Silicon Valley Mathematics Initiative, and Spencer Foundation have also provided important funding for the lesson study initiatives described in this handbook. The Abe Fellowship Program of the Social Science Research Council and the American Council of Learned Societies, with funds provided by the Japan Foundation's Center for Global Partnership, funded the work in Japan.

This book is also made possible by the generosity of many, many educators and researchers who have shared their lesson study work with us over the past fifteen years. We can name only a few of them.

Mary Pat O'Connell was the coinitiator of Lesson Study in San Mateo-Foster City School District. She saw its potential immediately, back in 1999, and has never stopped strategizing about how to improve lesson study and how to use it to improve education. Her unequivocal support, as principal, colleague, and friend, and her patient, long-range vision for lesson study implementation has kept the work moving forward in our region. The long hours we have spent with her, planning, problem solving, and pushing each other's ideas about professional learning, resonate through all parts of this book. Likewise, from the start, mathematics coaches Barbara Scott and April Cherrington saw the potential of lesson study to meet the professional learning needs of teachers and helped figure out how to grow and sustain lesson study across schools.

David Foster has, from the very beginning, championed the work described in this book, providing important leadership, guidance, resources, and inspiration that allowed the work to grow from site-based pockets to a regional network. His willingness to put his own practice on view in large public research lessons, while juggling all the demands of his work as a foundation officer, remain for us a touchstone of real leadership.

Heather Chang, Diane Gee, Linda Bauld, Carolyn Bosque, and Ellie Shields, the teacher participants in the "How Many Seats" DVD, bravely and generously allowed us to video record their fledgling lesson study work during an intensive two-week summer institute. Their willingness to share the real challenges of this work with a broad audience has done much to build our images of lesson study and our images of learning within our profession. We were fortunate to partner with Peter Shwartz of DellaRuth Studios in this endeavor, whose technical acumen and educational vision both shaped the DVD.

Monika Hastings, Linette Giffiths, Tami Wong, Lisa Brown, Suzi Riley, and Jane Danbold, the teachers and coaches of the "Improving Writing Through Lesson Study" DVD, allowed us to follow and document their work for a year, sharing the hard conversations and process involved in improving our practice. Joe Young, a technology magician and teacher, created the YouTube and DVD materials, so that other teachers could learn from this work.

Members of the Mills College Lesson Study Group have contributed over many years, in central ways, to the ideas and materials in this handbook. Dr. Rebecca Perry meticulously and thoughtfully—but somehow not invasively—documented the early lesson study work in San Mateo-Foster City on video and through interviews. Her examination of the work, questions about it, and feedback of results substantially improved and deepened lesson study practice in San Mateo-Foster City. Rebecca has been central in the development of many of the tools, frameworks, and ideas central to this book, and would be a coauthor were it not for her crucial role in managing MCLSG's research arm. Likewise, Shelley Friedkin has been an important colleague since her days as project coordinator, deftly pulling together large lesson study institutes and organizing mountains of video and documents so that she could somehow find any piece we were looking for and answer any question put to her. We were worried as she moved toward completion of her doctorate, since we figured no one could fill her shoes, but Melissa Crockett has proven us wrong. Both Shelley and Melissa made important contributions to editing the Highlands School video linked to this book.

We have a particular debt to the many teachers, alas too numerous to list here, who have pioneered lesson study in the Bay Area and beyond. Teachers opened their classrooms to colleagues, took leadership at their sites, and built practices of public observation and analysis of teaching and learning, thereby changing the culture of our profession. They fashioned a model of lesson study that could be sustained and replicated in our region. They brought to life lesson study through hard work, passion, and a willingness to challenge themselves in order to provide the best possible learning experience for students. We are particularly grateful for the steady contributions over many years of Lucy de Anda, Elizabeth Baker, Linda Fisher, Alice Gill, Jane Gorman, Bill Jackson, Lynn Liptak, Aki Murata, Stan Pesick, Phil Tucher, Ineko Tsuchida, Shelly Weintraub, the Willard Middle School Lesson Study Group, and teachers of the San Mateo-Foster City School District.

This book is also made possible by the extraordinary generosity of our Japanese colleagues who have opened up their practice of lesson study and, on many occasions, rolled up their sleeves to help us do the work of adapting lesson study to the United States. Their numbers are too great to thank every one individually, but we would like to specifically acknowledge the contributions of three Japanese educators residing in the United States who have greatly shaped the face of lesson study in this country over the past twelve years: Akihiko Takahashi, Tad Watanabe, and Makoto Yoshida. We would also like to acknowledge the contributions to our understanding of lesson study made by Kiyomi Akita, Toshiakira Fujii, Fumio Hiramatsu, Kyoko Ishii, Kyoichi Itoh, Mayumi Ito, Masami Kajijta, Eiji Morita, Yasuhiko Nakano, Shigefumi Nagano, Katsumi Ninomiya, Yukinobu Okada, Hiroko Oomasa, Manabu Sato, Yoshinori Shimizu, Yoshishige Sugiyama, Hiroshi Tanaka, Kozo Tsubota and the entire faculties of Iwanishi Elementary School, Kitaissha Elementary School, Komae Elementary School Number Seven, Sendagaya Elementary School, Takamiminami Elementary School, and Gakugei, Shizuoka, and Tsukuba Affiliated Elementary Schools.

Catherine wishes to thank the members of the School of Education at Mills College and the Mills College Children's School colleagues, who epitomize the many benefits of working together to improve practice. She also wishes to thank her husband, Andy Leavitt, and her sons, Daniel and Matthew Leavitt, who have brought many interesting questions and insights to the topic of lesson study, as well as great patience and support. She dedicates this work to Andy, with a renewed promise to excavate the bedroom.

Jackie wishes to thank her son and daughter, Sean and Erin, and amazing husband, Jack. They are her center and greatest support and make her proud and content. She also wants to thank her sister Michele, who helps her keep things in perspective, and whose dedication to education inspires Jackie to be a better teacher. Jackie dedicates this book to her good friend Ellie Shields (1949–2008), who loved lesson study and loved teaching. Ellie epitomized what it was to be a good teacher; she loved to learn, reflect, and think deeply about practice. She was always looking for ways to improve learning and kept her eye keenly on what matters most, children.

intro

Introduction:
What Is Lesson Study?

Improving something as complex and culturally embedded as teaching requires the efforts of all the players, including students, parents, and politicians. But teachers must be the primary driving force behind change. They are best positioned to understand the problems that students face and to generate possible solutions.

—JAMES STIGLER AND JAMES HIEBERT, *THE TEACHING GAP* (1999, 135)

Lesson study is an approach to instructional improvement that has spread rapidly in North America since the first published description in 1997 (Lewis and Tsuchida 1997). Figure I–1 provides an overview of the lesson study cycle, during which teachers work together to:

- Consider their goals for student learning and long-term development and identify gaps between these long-term goals and current reality.

- Identify a pressing issue in student learning, examine research and curriculum related to that issue, and collaboratively choose or plan a "research lesson" to study and advance instruction with respect to this issue.

- Conduct the research lesson, with one team member teaching and others gathering data on student learning and development.

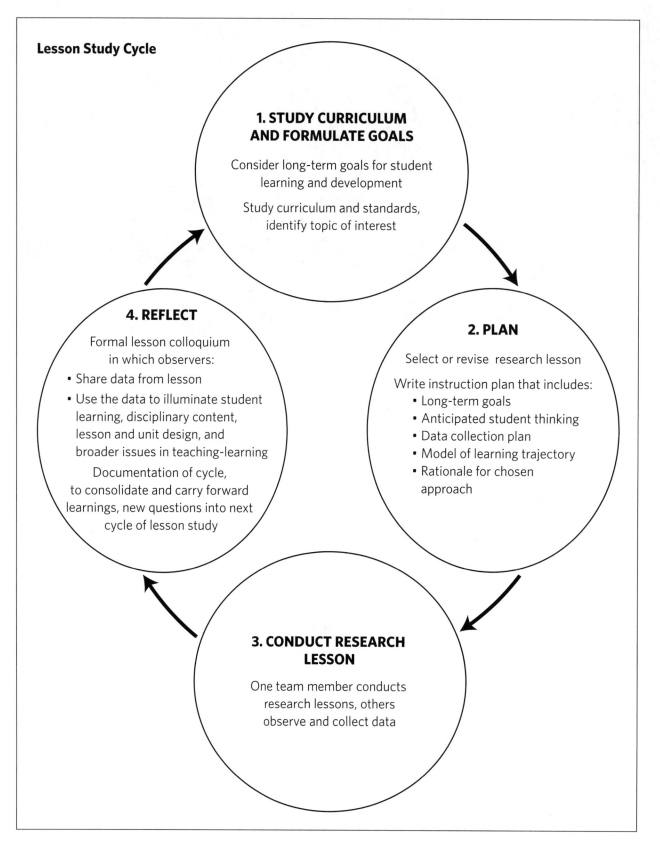

Lesson Study Cycle

1. STUDY CURRICULUM AND FORMULATE GOALS

Consider long-term goals for student learning and development

Study curriculum and standards, identify topic of interest

2. PLAN

Select or revise research lesson

Write instruction plan that includes:
- Long-term goals
- Anticipated student thinking
- Data collection plan
- Model of learning trajectory
- Rationale for chosen approach

3. CONDUCT RESEARCH LESSON

One team member conducts research lessons, others observe and collect data

4. REFLECT

Formal lesson colloquium in which observers:
- Share data from lesson
- Use the data to illuminate student learning, disciplinary content, lesson and unit design, and broader issues in teaching-learning

Documentation of cycle, to consolidate and carry forward learnings, new questions into next cycle of lesson study

Figure I–1 The Lesson Study Cycle

- Share and discuss the data gathered during the lesson, drawing out implications for lesson and unit design and for teaching and learning more broadly.
- If desired, revise the lesson, teach it in another classroom, and study and improve it again.[1]

Lesson study is a simple idea. If you want to improve instruction, what could be more obvious than collaborating with fellow teachers to plan instruction and examine its impact on students? Although the idea may be simple, lesson study is a complex process. In lesson study, teachers work together in ways that may be unfamiliar, for example, to challenge and build one another's knowledge of subject matter and of student thinking and to observe in one another's classrooms. Teachers focus on student thinking, rather than on teaching moves, and question and investigate the impact of lessons—rather than assuming that lessons work because they are from "proven" or mandated programs.

This handbook highlights strategies used by successful lesson study groups to make the work of lesson study productive, safe, and inclusive. When lesson study is proposed, many educators are initially reluctant to have their teaching observed by colleagues. The protocols for observation and data collection assembled in this book have enabled teachers in many U.S. settings to reshape local educational culture—by building the expectation that teachers will observe in one another's classrooms and the know-how to facilitate productive conversations, focused on student thinking and learning.

Lesson Study and the Qualities of Effective Professional Learning

Figure I–2 lists qualities of effective professional learning identified by researchers. As you read about lesson study, you will probably note the many ways that it exemplifies these qualities of effective professional learning. It occurs in a real, motivating context—the classroom—and focuses on a problem of great interest to teachers: their shared goals for student learning and development. The research lesson provides an ongoing method to improve instruction, ensuring that good ideas are not just talked about but brought to life for shared observation and analysis. To plan research lessons, teachers draw on expertise from within and outside the school. They study particular academic content and gather the best lessons and instructional techniques from the nation (or world), improving them through careful observation of their own students. Lesson study builds collaboration as teachers progressively improve lessons that are "our" lessons, not "my" lessons.

---

1. Reteaching the research lesson is optional, but is recommended by Makoto Yoshida, a pioneer of lesson study in U.S. schools (see "A Closer Look," page 63).

Effective Professional Learning

- Is intensive, ongoing, and connected to practice
- Focuses on student learning and addresses the teaching of specific curriculum content
- Aligns with school improvement priorities and goals
- Builds strong working relationships among teachers

Source: Darling-Hammond, Wei, Andree, Richardson, and Orphanos (2009)

Figure I–2 Qualities of Effective Professional Development

What You'll Find in This Book

Chapter One explains the rationale for lesson study. We explore the ways in which lesson study values teachers and their professional community as well as the long-term academic and social development of students. Lesson study provides an important new learning structure—the research lesson—where teachers (often working in collaboration with subject matter specialists) can develop and improve a shared vision of good instruction. Through the careful observation and analysis of instruction, lesson study enables teachers to build professional knowledge that is directly useable in teaching and that can be spread, adapted, and improved upon (Hiebert, Gallimore, and Stigler 2002).

Chapter Two introduces lesson study with two examples. The accompanying DVD allows you to explore video of the mathematics lesson study cycle "How Many Seats?" in which a group of teachers from several different schools take part in lesson study during a summer mathematics institute. They develop, teach, observe, redesign, and reteach a research lesson designed to bring ideas from the institute to life in the classroom. In the process, these teachers deepen their knowledge of mathematics and teaching and their professional community. The second example, in language arts, is taken from the schoolwide lesson study work of Highlands Elementary School, in San Mateo, California. We follow teachers as they develop schoolwide goals for lesson study focused on reducing the achievement gap at their school and as group members choose a research-based teaching strategy to study and test in their research lessons.[2]

Chapters Three Through Five provide guidance through each step of the lesson study process, from building a lesson study group and homing in on a topic to

2. The four video segments for the Highland School lesson study are available to view on both YouTube and on Teacher Tube: www.youtube.com/watch?v=ZYAI05wpu6c, www.youtube.com/watch?v=Ivfjp4Nrwg0, www.youtube.com/watch?v=3GMmlEuajfk, www.youtube.com/watch?v=NRcKSjw1mpY and www1.teachertube.com/members/viewVideo.php?video_id=215796&title=SMFC, www1.teachertube.com/members/viewVideo.php?video_id=217289&title=SMFC, www1.teachertube.com/members/viewVideo.php?video_id=215801&title=SMFC, www1.teachertube.com/members/viewVideo.php?video_id=217292&title=SMFC.

preparing, conducting, and reflecting on a research lesson. We provide you with materials to support each step of the work, including a schedule for the overall process, sample meeting agendas, protocols for observation and discussion of lessons, templates for development of the research theme and teaching-learning plan, and suggested processes for norm setting and effective group management.

Chapter Six highlights eight opportunities central to lesson study. These include opportunities to build knowledge about teaching, about subject matter, and about students; to think carefully about the goals for teaching particular lessons and topics as well as long-term goals for students; to see one's own teaching through the eyes of students and colleagues; and to build professional community.

Chapter Seven explores eight different types of lesson study. These include small groups of volunteers (who have been the pioneers of lesson study in many parts of the United States); schools that practice lesson study schoolwide; subject matter associations that include regional or national lesson study components; and lesson study in education of preservice educators. Lesson study takes on somewhat different characteristics, and has somewhat different benefits, in each context. The full potential of lesson study in the United States will be fulfilled only when a diverse ecology of lesson study types emerges, so that local, regional, and national groups can build on and spread each other's unique contributions.

Chapter Eight addresses frequently asked questions about lesson study, including questions related to scheduling, facilitation, evaluation, and research evidence on the impact of lesson study. It also addresses common misconceptions about the nature of lesson study—for example, the misconception that lesson study produces a library of perfect lessons that are then disseminated.

Chapter Nine addresses challenges that face individual lesson study groups and the lesson study movement as a whole, including the need for a continued self-critical stance, for sharing across sites, and for connection with systemic change efforts.

Chapter Nine explores the benchmarks of mature lesson study and highlights how lesson study might provide a public proving ground for educators in the United States to build enactment of common core state standards.

Why Lesson Study?

On day two of working with my lesson study team, I thought this was really hard work, I was going to give up. But now, I am seeing and learning so much that I never could have gotten on my own. It is exciting that we are all learning together.

—HEIDI YAMADA, FOURTH-GRADE TEACHER, MENLO PARK, CALIFORNIA

At a time when so many school districts are already suffering from reform overload, why is lesson study important? This chapter highlights five features that enable lesson study to build sustained professional learning within schools and across the profession.

1. **Lesson study values teaching, teachers, and the professional teaching community** and cultivates all of these to sustain instructional improvement.

2. **Lesson study provides an important new learning structure—the research lesson**—where teachers gather data to inform improvement. The research lesson brings together the ideas of teachers, researchers, and policy makers.

3. **Lesson study values the *long-term* learning and development of students** and helps teachers build students' academic learning *and* their development of important qualities such as curiosity and persistence that will continue to improve student learning over time.

4. **Lesson study fosters teachers' intrinsic motivation** to continue to improve their own teaching and that of colleagues.

5. **Lesson study builds a shared knowledge base** for teaching that can be tested and refined.

1 Lesson Study Values Teaching, Teachers, and the Professional Teaching Community

The most brilliant educational visions are just splotches of ink on paper until a teacher somewhere brings them to life in a classroom. Lesson study recognizes the central importance and difficulty of teaching—of actually bringing to life standards, frameworks, and "best practices" in the classroom. Lesson study is a system of research and development in which teachers help to refine ideas about "best practice" through careful study of actual instruction. Lynn Liptak, one of the first U.S. principals to implement lesson study, contrasts traditional professional development with lesson study in Figure 1–1. As it shows, lesson study places teachers in an active role as researchers. As New Jersey teacher Heather Crawford (quoted in Lewis 2002, p. 15) noted:

> Lesson study is teacher-directed, teacher-driven. . . . It is really teacher-oriented. Most other professional development is like a seminar. You sit there and you listen. You may do a little bit of hands-on stuff, but usually they are just feeding you information. Here, we are seeking our own information. We are doing our own research.

"One-size-fits-all" professional development rarely meets the needs of all teachers within a school or district. In lesson study, teachers bring their own pressing questions to the table. In the same lesson study group, a new teacher may learn basic strategies to elicit and manage student writing while an experienced team member learns about recent developments in the teaching of nonfiction writing. Participants in a lesson study group seek out answers from one another, from outside specialists and research, and from careful study of students during a lesson that incorporates teachers' collective knowledge.

TRADITIONAL	LESSON STUDY
Begins with answer	Begins with question
Driven by outside "expert"	Driven by participants
Communication flow: trainer → teachers	Communication flow: among teachers
Hierarchical relations between trainer and learners	Reciprocal relations among learners
Research informs practice	Practice is research

By Lynn Liptak, Paterson School No. 2, New Jersey

Figure 1–1 Contrasting Views of Professional Development

What is the evidence that lesson study improves student achievement?

There is a growing body of evidence that lesson study and closely related practices improve student learning (Lewis et al. 2006; Lewis, Perry, and Hurd 2009; Foster and Poppers 2009; Saunders, Goldenberg, and Gallimore 2009; Perry and Lewis 2010; Waterman 2011). These studies also provide a plausible explanation of how and why lesson study improves student learning, through increases in teachers' knowledge of content and pedagogy, focus on student thinking, and mutual respect for instructional improvement. Lesson study builds a professional learning community in which teachers improve their knowledge of content, teaching, and students and their belief that changes in their own teaching can help students learn. Accountability to colleagues, focus on student learning, and continued efforts to improve are natural and integral parts of the teacher learning community that develops in lesson study.

Planning instruction is a comfortable and familiar activity for teachers. Teachers naturally want to plan lessons that reach students well. So lesson study uses a familiar routine (planning lessons) to draw out teachers' knowledge and help them examine and extend their knowledge—in a powerful fashion that one of our colleagues dubbed "differentiated learning for teachers." During research lessons, teachers are often surprised to discover how much thinking and learning students can do. And so lesson study may help us think in new ways about students.

Advancing the Profession While Remaining in the Classroom

Lesson study also provides a path for advancement within teaching that does not entail leaving the classroom. The Japanese classroom teachers most actively involved in lesson study regularly attract thousands of educators to their research lessons (large video screens and speakers are used to project the lesson to the audience), and they write widely read books on their lesson study work. A culture of large public lessons is beginning to emerge in the United States, as well, with annual lessons now occurring in several locations across the country.[1] Teachers active in these large public settings can influence education widely through their public research lessons and writing, yet keep their feet firmly planted in the realities of classroom life.

Stop the Revolving Door

It has been noted that the United States suffers not from a shortage of qualified teachers but from an inability to keep them in teaching. Each year, teachers

---

1. For example, public lessons have been conducted for a number of years by the Sonoma County Office of Education (www.scoe.org/pub/htdocs/lesson-study.html), the Chicago Lesson Study Group (www.lessonstudygroup.net), the Silicon Valley Mathematics Initiative (www.svmimac.org/lessonstudy.html), and Global Education Resources (www.globaledresources.com/events.html).

face a proliferation of new mandates, ideas, and materials. In the midst of such overwhelming demands, lesson study enables teachers to focus on an issue of importance and study it carefully with colleagues, in an actual classroom. The collective sense of efficacy developed by working with colleagues in lesson study—the sense that, working together, we can figure out solutions to our challenges—may provide an important antidote to the problem of teacher burnout. Research suggests that it is lack of a collegial work environment that leads teachers to leave the profession, more than any other factor, including salary (Brill and McCartney 2008).

Changing School Culture

As lesson study brings together teachers to study and solve problems, it re-shapes school culture. Teachers develop a common language as they collectively identify and tackle problems. Teachers reveal their individual interpretations of educational jargon and work collaboratively to understand how new ideas should look in practice. Talk around the copy machine and in the lunch room changes. As lesson study work seeps into school culture, it becomes the norm for teachers to ask each other how particular lessons went in the classroom and what changes are needed. A basic premise of lesson study is that there is always more to learn about the practice of teaching. Teachers are able to admit that they do not have all the answers. Over time, lesson study creates a friendlier working environment and a radical change in the culture of a school. Teachers who participate in lesson study report that learning with colleagues is effective and enjoyable more than do comparison teachers who do not participate (Lewis and Perry 2010).

2 Lesson Study Provides an Important New Learning Structure—The Research Lesson

The United States now has various standards designed to improve classroom instruction, including "common core state standards" shared across many states. How are these standards best brought to life in classrooms? Lesson study assumes that something more than posting standards on the classroom blackboard or having administrators walk through classrooms is needed. Lesson study assumes that teachers need opportunities to work with colleagues to bring the standards to life in actual lessons, carefully study the student thinking that results, and revisit the meaning and approach to the standard in light of actual instruction. Outside content specialists or university-based educators often participate in lesson study as well, bringing into the process new perspectives and recent research. Well-designed research lessons provide a place for teachers to bring to life their understanding of good instruction, based on careful, collaborative study of existing materials and research. It provides a forum for teachers, researchers, and administrators to see how their ideas cohere or differ and to identify points for future discussion and development. "A Closer Look" provides a vivid example of the power of live research lessons that bring together teachers, subject matter specialists, and administrators.

A Closer Look: What Is Problem Solving?

The power of shared, live examples of standards-based instruction was brought home to us in 2001, when Akihiko Takahashi taught the public lesson "How to Open a Cube" in a San Mateo classroom. (The teaching-learning plan is included in Appendix A and video segments of this lesson can be viewed at www.lessonresearch.net.) The lesson brought to life ideas about problem solving that have developed through decades of lesson study collaboration between Japanese classroom teachers and mathematicians.

Problem solving is of course a key element in most mathematics standards, including those in California. In the discussion following the research lesson, we found something startling. Many of the nearly one hundred educators who observed the lesson thought it epitomized the experiences needed to foster problem-solving skills and habits of mind; yet, a few observers, including some influential state policy makers, could not see any relationship between the lesson and mathematical standards! For example, some educators commented that they thought the many references to "problem solving" in the California mathematics framework referred to solving word problems related to previously learned content, not to solving novel problems like the one presented in the lesson. By bringing to life his vision of problem solving, Dr. Takahashi prompted others to share their own ideas about the nature of mathematical "problem solving" and the experiences that foster it and to compare the lesson task and student thinking they had just seen with what occurred routinely in their own classrooms. Attending educators were amazed to find out that they had interpreted "problem solving" in the state mathematics standards so differently from some of their colleagues. The research lesson sparked educators in this region of California to begin to negotiate a shared understanding and body of knowledge about problem solving.

. . . .

Shifting the Weight of Instructional Improvement

In the United States, we tend to spend a great deal of time writing standards and relatively little time observing and refining the classroom lessons designed to bring these ideas to life. Lesson study researcher Clea Fernandez (Lewis 2002, p. 8) comments on U.S. reform:

> When reform ideas fail to move from rhetoric to action, we often interpret this as a failure to communicate the ideas clearly, and we revise and improve the documents. It is as if we feel that if we can find just the right set of words and examples telling teachers what to do in their classrooms, they will act accordingly.

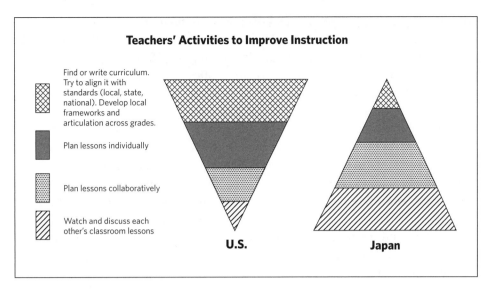

Teachers' Activities to Improve Instruction

Find or write curriculum. Try to align it with standards (local, state, national). Develop local frameworks and articulation across grades.

Plan lessons individually

Plan lessons collaboratively

Watch and discuss each other's classroom lessons

U.S.   Japan

Figure 1–2 Instructional Improvement Time in the United States and Japan

Figure 1–2 schematically illustrates the use of instructional improvement time in the United States and Japan. Many factors conspire to keep U.S. teachers in the top layer of the triangle, where they spend their time articulating what will be taught at each grade level, finding curricula, trying to align curricula with state or district standards, and writing lessons to fill the resulting holes. Although these may be needed activities, they do not reveal what actually happens in classrooms. The triangle of U.S. instructional improvement thus stands precariously on its tip; we are trying to improve instruction without actually observing and discussing it. In contrast, Japanese instructional improvement rests on a solid base of observation, discussion, and refinement of classroom lessons. Lesson study provides a way to shift emphasis from the top layer of Figure 1–2 to the base, so that our instructional improvement efforts rest on a substantial base of lesson observation and improvement.

Data That Illuminate Learning

We are often told that school reform should be guided by data. Unfortunately, the "data" often consist of test results that do little to illuminate the process of learning and how it might be improved. In contrast, during research lessons teachers carefully observe students and collect data to answer questions like the following:

- Did students use the knowledge learned in previous grades?
- What elements of lesson design supported student learning, and what served as barriers?
- How did students' knowledge and understanding of the topic change over the course of the lesson and unit?
- Did students show the basic habits and skills needed for learning, such as organization, persistence, and ability to listen and respond to one another's ideas?

In a process very similar to the "quality circles" credited for improvement of manufacturing, teachers analyze these data and use them as a basis to design changes in instruction and, more generally, in classroom practices and approaches.

Although tests and student work may offer information on *what* to improve, lesson study also sheds light on *how* to improve; it yields what Lee Shulman has called "low-stakes, high-yield" assessment data (Shulman 2007). For example, team members might notice that the manipulative used to teach a particular concept is misunderstood by students and devise a better one. In contrast to standardized tests, feedback from lesson study is immediate, specific to the school's curriculum and goals, and based on actual observation of the lesson and students. It comes from colleagues likely to have intimate knowledge of the students and their context, the people "best positioned to understand the problems that students face and to generate possible solutions" (Stigler and Hiebert 1999).

Educators have noted that knowledge useful to practitioners often differs from typical research knowledge in three ways:

1. It is linked with practice.

2. It is concrete, detailed, and specific.

3. It is organized and integrated around problems of practice (Hiebert, Gallimore, and Stigler 2002).

Because lesson study centers on the observation and analysis of actual practice, it yields such knowledge.

3 Lesson Study Values the *Long-Term* Learning and Development of Students

Think of a classroom you know. Imagine what would happen if every child arrived at the beginning of the year well organized, eager to uphold class rules, able to get along well with others, and highly motivated to learn. What difference would it make in what you could teach? The personal qualities that are fundamental to success in school, such as persistence, responsibility, and desire to learn, develop over many years, in many classrooms. As an elementary teacher explained, teachers cannot greatly improve children's lives *except* by working together as a whole faculty to provide a coherent, consistent environment for children's development of these qualities. What's the use if children learn to "think like scientists" in one classroom, only to have those qualities devalued by next year's teacher?

Lesson study does not just target academic development. It also scrutinizes motivation and social climate, factors likely to contribute heavily to students' long-term academic success (Solomon et al. 2000). It focuses on the basic habits and personal qualities that contribute to student motivation and learning and reshapes many elements of school life to promote those qualities. Do students use and build upon each other's ideas during discussions, take careful notes, work effectively with group mates, and take initiative as learners? These are all qualities that can be built as part of the lesson study research theme (see Chapter Four).

The long-term focus of lesson study may also help prevent pendulum swings between the social and academic goals of education (Lewis and Tsuchida 1997). When teachers look at instruction simultaneously through the lenses of promoting important personal qualities *and* academic learning, it is likely they will attend to both, rather than teaching in ways that inadvertently undermine one or the other. Research shows that meeting students' needs for belonging and contribution at school, if done well, boosts students' academic development by promoting students' positive attachment to school.[2] Long-term goals that emphasize both social and academic development may help guard against the "quick fixes" that temporarily boost students' test performance while undermining their subsequent motivation to learn and their identification with school.

4 Lesson Study Fosters Teachers' Motivation to Continue to Improve

It has been said that American education suffers not from a shortage of good programs, but from a lack of demand for them (Elmore 1999–2000). Ironically, the lively Japanese science lessons that first interested Catherine in lesson study were based in part on model U.S. science lessons brought back to Japan by Japanese educators who visited the United States! Japanese educators spread the U.S. approaches throughout Japan, improving on them and adapting them to local needs through lesson study. Lesson study supports teachers' natural inclination to improve instruction and allows them to take initiative—rather than feeling "done to."

Lesson study also ups the ante on what is considered good teaching. No one requires teachers to adopt the research lessons they see. But good new approaches tend to spread quickly. During a research lesson, if you see students gasp in amazement when they measure circles of various sizes and discover that the circumference is always a little more than three times as long as the diameter, you will want to give your own students the thrill of discovering pi in this way. When you see students in the classroom next door eagerly applying narrative writing revision strategies that your students ignore, you want to know how you can build the same learning in your classroom. Research lessons create a natural, grassroots demand among teachers to improve teaching, and they provide a concrete, shared example of the educational visions that might otherwise be just buzzwords. Too often, we ask teachers to do something they've never seen or experienced. It shouldn't be a surprise that teachers apply innovative curricula in traditional ways, if they have not had the chance to see the innovation in a classroom, with students responding in real time.

Too often, educational improvement focuses on new magic bullets, as if just the right curriculum or teaching strategy will singlehandedly accomplish miraculous change. Lesson study assumes that educational improvement entails

---

2. Research suggests that schools *can* promote both social and academic development effectively if they use intrinsic motivation, rather than competition, to foster academic development. See, for example, Lewis, Schaps, and Watson (1995, 1999) and Solomon et al. (2000).

steady, ongoing work by teachers to examine new as well as old ideas and to study carefully how they can be made to work in the classroom. A sense of efficacy and urgency on the part of teachers are central to this work. A California middle school teacher reflected on lesson study: "I am repeatedly invigorated and challenged by my colleagues' honesty and their own desire for growth inspires the same in me." A fifth-grade California teacher said, "Lesson study . . . has the potential for empowering teachers by demonstrating to them their own ability to improve their practice and the learning of their students."

5 Lesson Study Builds a Knowledge Base for Teaching

James Stigler and James Hiebert (1999) argue in *The Teaching Gap* that lesson study supplies a key missing element in reform: a means to improve teaching and learning through development of a shared professional knowledge base on teaching. Through live research lessons, written reports, videos, and networking with colleagues, lesson study builds and spreads knowledge about teaching and learning, creating a system that learns. The teachers in the accompanying video "How Many Seats?" learned, for example, about the usefulness of careful observation of student counting methods and about the power of having students organize data themselves, rather than be given a chart to organize it. The knowledge gained from this cycle spread easily to other individuals and settings, as these teachers informally talked about their work, showed the lesson videos at institutes, and actively experimented in their own classrooms to discover the impact of worksheets on other mathematical tasks. Careful observation of student counting methods quickly became a routine habit for teachers participating in lesson study. Teachers often referenced "How Many Seats?" when discussing whether a lesson could be redesigned to better challenge students.

The knowledge base built through lesson study includes knowledge about student thinking, lesson design, and teaching strategies. After discovering that the manipulatives used to teach subtraction did not allow teachers to reconstruct students' thinking, teachers in a Japanese lesson study group developed a list of characteristics of a good manipulative and systematically set about redesigning the manipulative to teach subtraction (Fernandez and Yoshida 2004). A group of elementary teachers discovered that students proposed very different strategies for lifting a 220-pound sack when asked to look at an *actual* sack than when given an *illustration* of the sack on a worksheet—an insight that has spread to many teachers who have seen video of that lesson study cycle.[3] "A Closer Look" offers a powerful example of how knowledge for teaching can spread across a region through lesson study.

The Lesson Is Not the Product

As should be clear by now, lesson study is not primarily about producing a lesson. It is about developing the knowledge, dispositions, relationships, and windows into

---

3. "Can You Lift 100 Kilograms?" is an eighteen-minute video of the lesson study cycle in a Japanese school, available from www.lessonresearch.net.

A Closer Look: The Spread of Reengagement Through a Regional Lesson Study Network

Although lesson study is still in its infancy in the United States, in our region of California we have already seen some examples of knowledge built and spread through lesson study. In 2002, Linda Fisher, director of the Noyce Foundation's regional mathematics assessment collaborative, participated in a series of research lessons taught by Dr. Akihiko Takahashi, an experienced Japanese elementary teacher (now an associate professor at DePaul University). Fisher was struck by Takahashi's public use of student work to help students make connections between different solution methods and to consider common misconceptions; it seemed Takahashi "slowed down" the lesson and probed student thinking during the discussion, a process the Japanese call *neriage* (polishing or kneading) (Takahashi 2008).

Linda Fisher decided to work on *neriage* in her own practice. When she subsequently taught a public research lesson in front of more than fifty mathematics coaches, she carefully planned the types and order of student strategies to be shared with the class and the specific connections she would try to help students make among the solution strategies. She taught a preliminary version of the lesson to another class and studied their solutions, in order to have the opportunity for careful planning in advance of the public research lesson. She dubbed the strategy of presenting student work for discussion "reengagement," because the discussion reengages students in thinking about mathematics they have studied.

When the coaches saw the level of discussion Linda was able to evoke, many of them began to experiment with reengagement in their own lesson study work, customizing it to their own purposes. From 2002 through the present, reengagement has spread through a regional lesson study network to teachers in many districts.[4] For example, after finding that peer discussions sometimes led students to abandon correct solutions in favor of incorrect solutions advocated by a peer, teachers at Willard Middle School, in Berkeley, California, used reengagement as a way to revisit problematic issues such as confusion of additive and proportional reasoning. Teachers in Emery, California, used reengagement as a way to help second graders reflect on the evidence included in a good solution, and teachers in San Mateo used it to reintroduce and analyze common errors from a prior lesson. As teachers shared their research lessons and their learning from the lessons, they accumulated considerable knowledge about how to use reengagement.

● ●

---

4. Silicon Valley Mathematics Initiative has been funded by The Noyce Foundation, Kabcenell Foundation, Santa Clara Valley Math Project, Silicon Valley Community Foundation, and contributions from forty public school districts in the greater San Francisco Bay Area. From the 2004–2005 school year, the Kabcenell Foundation also funded a lesson study network that brought together lesson study teams from fourteen to twenty districts for an annual conference (with research lessons) and for "exchange" research lessons between pairs of lesson study teams.

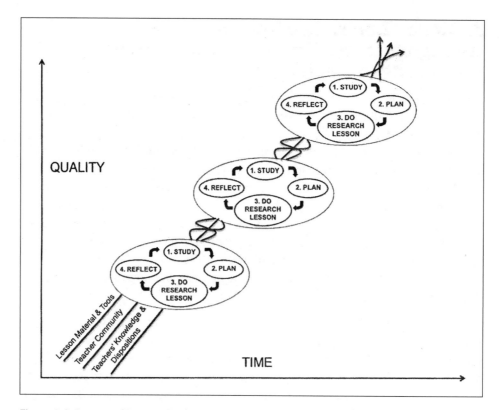

Figure 1–3 Impact of Lesson Study on Lesson Materials, Teacher Community, and Teacher Knowledge and Dispositions

each other's classrooms that we need to improve instruction and to make our schools places where we will all continue to learn. Figure 1–3 highlights the interwoven changes that occur over time, in individual teachers, the teacher learning community, and instructional materials and tools.

> One thing I am taking away from this experience is to spend time when I am planning a lesson, anticipating what students will do instead of just hoping. That way I'll spend a lot less time freezing up when they don't do what the book says.
>
> (MOOLANI NAPOLITANI, SECOND-GRADE TEACHER)

Why would you want to spend so much time planning just one lesson?

The real "product" of the lesson study cycle is not the lesson. Lesson study builds educators' knowledge, motivation, habits of learning, and professional learning community. Figure 1–3 illustrates how lesson study fosters, over time, the knowledge and learning dispositions of individual teachers, the development of the teacher learning community, and the improvement of instructional materials and tools—not just lesson plans, but also tools for observing and discussing instruction, setting norms, and so forth.

Each cycle of lesson study is like a pebble tossed into a lake, creating ripples of influence across a school, district, or region. Over time, these ripples can create change in the culture of a school, district, or whole educational system (Lewis and Tsuchida 1997). Teachers, working in small groups with their colleagues, naturally want to create the best instruction they can for their students. Knowledge that the collaboratively planned lesson will be taught in front of others creates a strong sense of accountability, an incentive to work through differences of opinion, and a desire to draw on the best available research knowledge.

Lesson Study in Action

Professional development that is going to make a difference to students in the classroom must be teacher driven and student focused. Lesson study is both of these things.

—PRINCIPAL LYNN LIPTAK, PATERSON PUBLIC SCHOOL NO. 2

The best way to learn about lesson study is to participate. In this chapter, we do the next best thing—participate vicariously. The first part of the chapter focuses on the accompanying video "How Many Seats?" which provides a twenty-minute introduction to lesson study, following a group of teachers as they conduct a lesson study cycle during a summer mathematics institute. The second part of this chapter examines the use of lesson study in schoolwide improvement, highlighting an elementary school that focused on improving student writing through lesson study.

How Many Seats?

Before reading the remainder of this chapter, we recommend that you view the video "How Many Seats?" after consulting the guide found in Appendix B. Whether you view the video on your own or with a group of colleagues, the guide includes helpful questions and ideas to frame your review of each video segment. As recommended in the guide, we also suggest that you solve the problem in Figure 2–1 and consider two questions: What strategies might students use? What mathematics do you hope students would learn from working on the problem?

The video "How Many Seats?" follows six participants in a two-week summer mathematics institute that incorporated lesson study. During the first few days of the institute, the teachers had solved and discussed algebra problems, studied the state mathematics standards, and considered the algebra found within elementary school mathematics. Facing a new mandate for all eighth graders to take algebra, this group of elementary and middle school teachers is keenly concerned about how their instruction can lay the foundation for students to succeed in algebra. Teachers work in cross-site, cross-grade teams to tackle this new mandate. Lesson study makes what could seem an enormous burden to an individual teacher an approachable task because teachers address it collectively, bringing together their talents and experiences.

1 Planning and Study

As the video begins, the team is selecting the focus for their research lesson. After discussing the kinds of mathematical skills and thinking needed to succeed in algebra, team members decide to focus on building students' capacity to identify patterns and represent them mathematically. As one team member explains: "I think students are pretty strong in seeing patterns, but not necessarily then going to the next step of establishing a rule and writing an equation, at least at this point, at the beginning of fourth grade. We don't always take them on to [ask] . . . 'How would we represent this with numbers?'" Another team member adds: "I would say that would be true for the beginning of fifth grade, too."

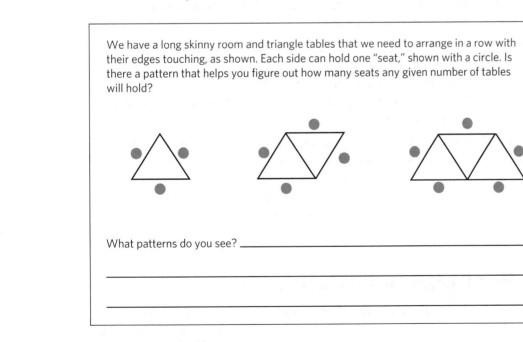

Figure 2-1 Seats Problem

After comparing lessons from several different textbooks, the teachers choose one textbook lesson as the basis for their research lesson, modifying it slightly to provide the real-world context of seats and tables (see Figure 2–1). Teachers focus their instructional planning on both a short-term goal—helping students learn to notice and mathematically represent patterns—and a long-term goal—for students to become curious, eager learners. Over the next ten days, the lesson study team works together through two cycles of planning, teaching, observing, discussing, and revising their research lesson.

2 First Teaching

On day six of the summer institute, one team member teaches the research lesson while the remaining team members and about a dozen invited outsiders (including several mathematics specialists) observe and take detailed notes on selected students. They note how each student's thinking progresses (or fails to) over the course of the lesson, and they document the supports and barriers to the student's learning. Following the lesson, the team members and outside observers participate in a postlesson discussion, during which they present and discuss the observational data they collected during the lesson.

This discussion surfaces an interesting contradiction: Most students correctly filled out the lesson worksheet (see Figure 2–2), but few students could express the connection between the plus-two pattern on the worksheet and the original problem of seats and tables, as the following excerpt from the end of the class reveals:

TEACHER: [*Asking class to guide her in writing the equation on the board*] The number of tables plus two equals what? [*Pauses, sees only a few hands raised*]

TEACHER: The number of tables plus two got us what? [*Pauses again, still sees relatively few hands raised*]

TEACHER: What are we trying to figure out? [*Pause*] What are we trying to figure out here? [*Pause*] We already know the number of tables. Jamie tells us we have to add two. What's that going to get us? [*Pause*] I'm not seeing many hands up. . . . The number of tables plus two equals what?

As the discussion following this lesson reveals, observing the first research lesson and collecting data on student learning are often transformative for teachers new to lesson study. The classroom becomes an arena for research, investigation, and reflection. Teachers begin to apply a new lens to their teaching—the lens of researcher (Fernandez, Cannon, and Chokshi 2003).

3 First Postlesson Discussion

As the teacher of the lesson reports, "At the very end, when I was trying to get them to say the number of tables plus two equals the number of seats, there was a lot of confusion. It's easy for them to just go plus two, plus two, plus two,

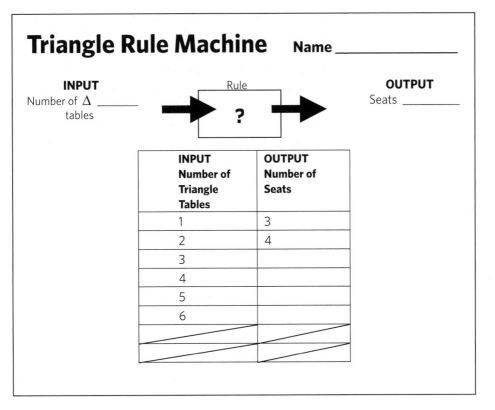

Figure 2–2 Seats Lesson Worksheet

and they sort of lose the whole picture of what the plus two is representing." She conjectures that the worksheet "spoon-fed" the pattern to the students, so that students easily saw the plus-two pattern in the chart but did not think through its connection to the problem.

Lesson study team members remark that if any one of them had taught this lesson alone in her classroom, it would have been easy to mistakenly conclude from students' easy and quick completion of the worksheets that they understood the pattern. But, because of the many sets of ears and eyes capturing students' working methods and speech during the lesson, and the public discussion of the observations, student learning is more carefully examined and an entirely different picture is revealed. What one teacher might have overlooked, the group detects: Many students do not see the connection between the plus-two pattern on the worksheet and the problem.

Revising the Lesson

The team decides to modify the lesson in several ways before reteaching it. They eliminate the worksheet and instead give each student a unique number of tables on a strip of paper, asking students to figure out the number of seats for that number of tables and to share data with tablemates in order to find a pattern that solves the problem. "It is in the messy business of organizing the data," predicts one team member, that students will understand the meaning of the mathematical pattern. The revised lesson also invites students to show classmates how they counted the seats. Team members hope that seeing different counting methods will help students notice that the "plus two" in the pattern is due to the "extra" seats at each end. This modification is sparked by the "big aha" of one team member who, during the first research lesson, observed a student counting one for each triangle base and one more for each end of the figure, revealing to the teacher the geometric reason for the "plus-two" pattern.

The team also modifies the lesson to have students create group posters reporting their data and what they discovered. The decision to add group posters stems from the team's discussion about how to move students to think more deeply—a discussion that calls upon teachers to share their strategies (thereby spreading knowledge across the profession). In fact, team members continue to experiment with the lesson after the institute. The following fall, when one member of the team teaches the lesson in her own classroom, she asks students to come to consensus on the mathematical patterns before writing them on the group poster. This modification stems from a problem noticed during the second research lesson— that some students failed to compare their discoveries with those of group mates, thereby missing an opportunity to discover errors in their own thinking.

The climate of the team is transformed after the teaching of the first lesson. The teammates are drawn together as the first lesson comes to fruition and team members develop shared insights. A bond is forming that allows the youngest member of the team, who has already agreed to teach the revised lesson, to take a risk and attempt a teaching strategy she has not tried before. Trusting the collective wisdom of the group, she agrees to get rid of the worksheets and give students nonsequential numbers, requiring students to organize and make sense of the data. She is willing to try this much more challenging lesson because the group shares responsibility for this decision.

4 & 5 Second Teaching and Second Postlesson Discussion

Two days after the first research lesson, the youngest team member teaches the revised research lesson to a different fourth-grade class. Once again, the remaining team members observe students and report their observations during a postlesson discussion. Their reports suggest that the redesigned lesson, in which students organized the data without support from a worksheet, better enabled students to understand and express the meaning of the mathematical patterns. For example, as students worked in their table groups, they frequently made comments such as "There's always two more seats than tables" and "There's one seat for each triangle, and one extra for each end."

During the postlesson discussion, one member of the team comments:

Having taught the first lesson, I would much rather have taught this lesson. Much rather. Because . . . the student-driven activities are so much more powerful. They discovered it. I wasn't pouring it into their ears. . . . It's their own personal information.

Another team member adds:

If you asked Monday's class to visualize their learning, they would probably visualize the worksheet and the plus two. Whereas in this class, they're going to remember . . . how different children counted and added the ends, or added two at each end [and one for each other triangle]. They owned it. The learning was so much more effective this time. It wasn't about teaching; it was about learning. To me, as a teacher, going back and looking at lessons and lesson plans, that idea can be used anywhere. To make sure that students are always the learners in the classroom. We're not necessarily the teachers.

Team members are very excited to see the improvement in student learning in response to the revised lesson. They see that students are capable of more challenging mathematics than they had thought, and they have a concrete picture of what they are striving for in their own classrooms. Seeing the improvement also inspires several team members to further revise the lesson and teach it in their own classrooms and to further investigate the impact of T-charts (like that provided in the original lesson) on students' thinking. For example, one team member tries two versions of a problem (with and without T-charts) within a lesson and discovers that, once again, the T-chart inhibits students' understanding.

6 Final Reflection

On the day following the second research lesson, the lesson study team writes up what they learned from teaching, revising, and reteaching the lesson. They concur that the second lesson gave them a better understanding of student thinking, and they discuss why:

JACKIE: What we were asking them about was less substantial in the first lesson than in the second lesson. . . . In the first lesson, we were asking them about the patterns on the chart. But in the second lesson, things weren't in a sequential order. So that was a harder thing for them to think about. . . . The thinking we were asking them to do [*in the first lesson*] was not so hard. So when you ask them about their thinking . . .

ELLIE: "Plus two, plus two, plus two" [*laughter*]. It was neater. . . . It was pretty neat and clean.

JACKIE: We're so good at that!

ELLIE: I always thought I loved it a lot. Until I watched the students' results, and I thought, "Ooh. You'd better get used to a different style [*of teaching*]." [*Laughter*]

JACKIE: So we did make them think more.

LINDA: Absolutely.

As the team continues to chronicle the changes they made to the research lesson and what they learned from making the changes, one team member suddenly remembers that they asked students to share their counting methods in the second lesson, a change not yet listed in their description of the second lesson. Teachers recall how students gained insight into the mathematical patterns in the problem by watching classmates count the sides, and one teacher remarks that she herself did not initially see the mathematical pattern or understand what students could learn from each other's counting methods:

LINDA: The focus on the counting. Having the kids talk about their counting—that was a big improvement. Because we started to talk about the process of what's happening here.

JACKIE: Having the students describe their counting really got at their thinking lot more, and it also made the lesson more accessible to other kids. It gave other kids a lot of opportunities to hear and think about what was going on in the lesson.

ELLIE: That's exactly right.

LINDA: And just a personal aha for me. When you had said . . . that we should really spend some time on having the students share [*their counting*], at first I thought, "Who cares about that?" I did not see that as an important thing because I personally did not see the pattern, that the ends are the plus two. I did not see that. So it just shows that in all this math, well in everything we teach, we're only as effective as our level of understanding. So we have to keep pushing ourselves to delve into . . . the why, the how come. That's the challenge.

Lesson Production Is Not the Primary Goal

Although lesson study is sometimes portrayed as a way to "polish" lessons, the case of "How Many Seats?" makes clear that team members plan and improve the lessons not as an end in itself, but as a way to deepen their own content knowledge, their knowledge of student thinking, their understanding of teaching and learning, and their commitment to improvement of their own practice and that of colleagues.

This example also shows how lesson study can begin to catalyze a change of culture. All but two of these teachers are from different schools and have not previously worked together. At the beginning of their lesson study work, they are cautious about sharing ideas, taking risks, and discussing what they know. But as they progress through the cycle, they learn that it can be safe and comfortable to learn together, and they taste the enjoyment of working together to build knowledge about teaching. They learn that lesson study is not about discovering the one right way to teach a lesson, but about building knowledge of many teaching strategies and habits of observation, inquiry, and analysis of practice.

Improving Student Writing: Schoolwide Lesson Study[1]

Our second lesson study example comes from Highlands Elementary School, which serves just over four hundred K–5 students in San Mateo-Foster City

---

1. A link to the video "Improving Student Writing Through Lesson Study," a thirty-minute, teacher-filmed video, is available at www.youtube.com/watch?v=ZYAl05wpu6c and www1.teachertube.com/members/viewVideo.php ?video_id=215796&title=SMFC. A guide for viewing the video and additional student writing samples are available at www.lessonresearch.net.

School District.[2] Jackie Hurd and three colleagues formed a small lesson study group during the 2000–01 school year and shared what they had learned from their lesson study work with the Highlands faculty in the spring of 2001.[3] Nearly all of the Highlands faculty decided to begin lesson study the following fall, and the remaining faculty joined the next year. Schoolwide lesson study continued through 2008, and, with changes in leadership and personnel, in pockets thereafter.

Creating a Common Research Theme

A schoolwide research theme chosen by the staff provides a common focus for the work of the different lesson study groups at Highlands. The research theme is a long-term goal—such as reduction of the achievement gap—agreed upon by the whole faculty of a school. (The process for developing a research theme is discussed in Chapter Four.) Each year, the staff reviews the research theme in light of what they have learned from their ongoing lesson study and any new challenges facing the school. Groups of three to six teachers, typically from the same or adjoining grade levels, form lesson study groups and regularly share their learning with the rest of the faculty, in the form of brief updates and research lessons.

In 2005, the Highlands staff was in its second year of investigating differentiation strategies. When the district mandated that schools focus on closing the achievement gap, teachers decided to use their ongoing lesson study of differentiation strategies to address the achievement gap at Highlands. During a site-based, district professional development day in September, the Highlands staff spent the first part of the morning reviewing student achievement data to identify the commonalities among the students who were not meeting benchmarks. Next, staff members used a "jigsaw" process to read and discuss four articles on strategies to close the achievement gap. These two activities laid the groundwork for the year's lesson study work. Building from where their lesson study work had left off the previous year, the faculty generated a research theme for the upcoming year: "How can we improve our use of effective integrated thematic instruction and differentiation strategies in order to help all students, and in particular our socioeconomically disadvantaged students, access their full potential and improve their performance relative to grade-level standards?" Although this research theme may seem like a mouthful to outsiders, for teachers at the school it signified that they would further deepen approaches that had proven useful (integrated thematic instruction and differentiation) and use them to address the pressing problem of the achievement gap.[4]

---

2. About half of Highland's students are non-Hispanic whites, 25 percent are Asian, 15 percent are Hispanic, 3 percent are African American, 4 percent are Filipino, and 4 percent are from other backgrounds; 17 percent of Highlands students are eligible for free or reduced lunch.

3. Funds included public (Eisenhower) money and private foundation funding (including funds from The Noyce Foundation, the Spencer Foundation, and the Silicon Valley Mathematics Initiative).

4. A link to the video is available at www.youtube.com/watch?v=ZYAI05wpu6c and www1.teachertube.com/members/viewVideo.php?video_id=215796&title=SMFC.

Applying New Knowledge in the Classroom

During the afternoon of the September professional development day, the staff broke into lesson study teams organized by content or grade-level interests; each team applied the schoolwide theme to their chosen content area and generated a hypothesis or question that they would like to address in their lesson study work. Several of the teachers in Jackie's team had recently attended a series of professional development institutes on the teaching of writing but found it challenging to get the desired impact when using the program's strategies in their classrooms. All but one of the teachers in this lesson study group had more than fifteen years of teaching experience, and all had participated at various times throughout their careers in professional development on the teaching of writing. Yet they all felt that they were struggling to implement an important instructional practice—writers' workshop. The teachers were enthusiastic about the strategies they had learned in the workshop, but struggled with day-to-day application of the strategies in the classroom, a type of professional learning gap for which lesson study can be very useful. The teachers invited two district literacy coaches, who were interested in learning about the process of lesson study, to work with them. Thus the team consisted of one teacher each from the first, third, and fourth grades, two second-grade teachers, and two coaches.

The group began by collecting baseline data on students' current writing. Each teacher had students write to an agreed-upon prompt and teachers scored these writing samples together, using a rubric that outlined students' strengths and weaknesses. (The teaching-learning plan and the rubric are provided in Appendixes C and D.) Teachers also identified the commonalities in the writing samples of their underperforming students across the grade levels. Next, the team reviewed the state and national standards for writing and chose narrative writing as an area of focus for their lesson study work, as it is a key genre at each grade level. Because the lesson study team spanned four grade levels, it provided a powerful opportunity for teachers to gain a broad perspective on the writing requirements across grade levels. Teachers of lower grades deepened their appreciation of the role they played in preparing students for the rigors of writing in upper-grade classrooms.

Coming to a Shared Understanding of "Modeling"[5]

The use of "touchstone books"—examples of exemplary writing for students to use as models for their own writing—was a strategy introduced in the professional development workshops the teachers had attended. Team members expressed frustration that although they were sharing samples of good writing with their students and calling attention to the authors' writing strategies, students did not incorporate these strategies in their own writing. A surprising discussion followed about "modeling" as a teaching strategy.

The use of the term *modeling* in education is very common; the teachers in the group assumed they understood what it meant. However, the coaches

---

5. A link to the video is available at www.youtube.com/watch?v=ZYAI05wpu6c and www1.teachertube.com/members/viewVideo.php?video_id=215796&title=SMFC.

pushed for a distinction between "using a model" (showing an exemplary piece of writing) and live "modeling" (thinking aloud while demonstrating writing in front of students). As teachers designed and taught a lesson in which the teacher provided a live, think-aloud "modeling" of strategies to improve writing—rather than simply a study of written "models"—the subtle but important difference between these two strategies became an important aha for teachers. The lesson study work allowed individual teachers to deepen their understanding of modeling, and it also created a more coherent shared understanding of this commonly used term.

Exploring Beliefs About the Achievement Gap[6]

As the work of the lesson study team progressed, the teachers often referred back to their research theme of investigating strategies that most effectively close the achievement gap. The discussions that occurred in the lesson study group pushed teachers to examine and reveal their own beliefs about the teacher's role in closing the achievement gap. Important beliefs that drive our practice can lie unexamined. Lesson study provides an opportunity for educators to air, test, and realign these beliefs.

Later in the school year, members of this team invited the rest of the staff to attend their second research lesson, in which the teacher modeled a strategy to improve her own narrative writing and team members collected data on the impact of the teacher's modeling on the writing of the underperforming students. Other members of the school staff were quite interested in the distinction between models and modeling, and they remarked on the implications for their own teaching. In addition, the research lesson sparked requests to have more teachers participate in professional development on the teaching of writing and to identify practices that could be consistently implemented at each grade level to maximize the success of students by fifth grade.

Implications Beyond One Lesson[7]

As the example from Highlands School illustrates, as teachers share their lesson study work, it can build "demand" for more participation in professional learning among teachers, instructional coherence across classrooms, and a schoolwide culture of learning from practice. Teachers can develop a collective sense of efficacy so that mandates like closing the achievement gap or building standards-based instruction feel less overwhelming. As Jackie noted: "The first year of lesson study, when we first did standards-based instruction, everyone said [the new California] standards weren't doable. But by the end of the year, it felt doable." As teachers think together about their long-term goals for students, share their struggles, and watch lessons in other classrooms, they become invested in the success of all students and in the quality of teaching throughout the school.

---

6. A link to the video is available at www.youtube.com/watch?v=lvfjp4Nrwa0 and www1.teachertube.com/members/viewVideo.php?video_id=217289&title=SMFC.

7. A link to the video is available at www.youtube.com/watch?v=3GMmIEuaijfk; www.youtube.com/watch?v=NRckSjw1mpY and www1.teachertube.com/members/viewVideo.php?video_id=215801&title=SMFC, www1.teachertube.com/members/viewVideo.php?video_id=217292&title=SMFC.

Lesson study has provided regular opportunities for Highlands teachers to make sense of knowledge from classroom observations and from research, to push one another's thinking about subject matter and its learning, and to develop a sense of mutual responsibility for students' learning. As one Highlands teacher commented, "It changes each one of us a little bit, thereby changing our whole school." Highlands' student achievement data suggest that lesson study is paying off for students as well. Over the years in which Highlands focused on mathematics lesson study, the multiyear net increase in state mathematics achievement test scores for students who remained at Highlands School was more than triple that for students who remained elsewhere in the district as a whole (Lewis et al. 2006).[8]

---

8. An increase of 91 scale score points compared to 26 points, a statistically significant difference ($F = .309$, $df = 845$, $p < .001$). To rule out competing hypotheses about causes of the increase, our colleague, Rebecca Perry, identified other reform efforts that Highlands participated in during 2001–2005 and identified all other elementary schools (five) that participated in these reform efforts. Gains in achievement for students who remained at each of these schools for longer than one year were compared with gains for all students who remained in the district. Only one school other than Highlands showed any statistically significant achievement gains relative to the district as a whole, and that school did not show sustained gains over three years. Although a causal connection between the achievement results and lesson study cannot be inferred from this nonexperimental study, other obvious explanations (such as changes in student populations served by the school and district) have been ruled out. Schoolwide lesson study appears to be a primary difference between the professional development at this school and other district schools during the years studied.

Build a Lesson Study Group

I would advise teachers who are just beginning to consider lesson study to forge ahead slowly. Lesson study is not something that one can "jump into." Understand what it entails. Don't skip any steps. . . . Understand that lesson study is about the process as much as it is about the lesson.

—NICK TIMPONE, TEACHER, HARLEM VILLAGE ACADEMY, NEW YORK CITY

In this chapter and the next few chapters, we turn our focus to the practical details of lesson study, providing information on each phase of the lesson study process, including how to:

- build a lesson study group (Chapter Three)
- focus the group's inquiry, study the topic, and plan the research lesson (Chapter Four)
- conduct and discuss the research lesson, reflect on what has been learned, and plan next steps (Chapter Five)

Figure 3–1 provides an overview of the lesson study process, including the number of meetings (of forty-five to ninety minutes) needed for each phase of the process. Just how much time each phase will take depends upon your particular group—your goals, familiarity with each other and with lesson study, whether you have good curriculum materials appropriate to your goals, and whether your research lesson will be taught and revised once, twice, or three times.

1.	**Build a lesson study group (one to two meetings).**

- Recruit members for a lesson study group (see Figure 3–2 for tips).
- Develop a shared understanding of lesson study.
- Share your ideas about high-quality professional learning, and use them to create ground rules for your group.
- Establish group norms.
- Make a specific time commitment and set a schedule of meetings.

2.	**Focus the group's inquiry (one to two meetings).**

- Agree on a research theme (main aim) that captures your long-term goals for students. If you are working in a schoolwide effort, do this as a whole school.
- Choose a subject area (e.g., science, social studies) if this is not already decided.
- Begin to identify a particular topic, unit, and lesson for study.

3.	**Study the topic and plan the research lesson (three to eight meetings).**

- Study standards, existing lessons, and research related to your unit/lesson of interest, consulting "knowledgeable others" if possible. If you need further information on student thinking, use a task or preliminary "dirty lesson" to gather it.
- Plan the research lesson, taking care to think about your long-term goals as well as your specific goals for the lesson and unit.
- Write a detailed teaching-learning plan, following the examples found in the appendixes. The teaching-learning plan helps anticipate student thinking, guide data collection, provide a rationale for lesson design, and record your questions and learnings.
- Write a data collection plan as part of the instructional plan, specifying the data to be collected.

4.	**Conduct and discuss the research lesson (one lesson period, with one-hour meeting same day or soon after; repeat if lesson is retaught).**

- Collect data as planned.
- Conduct a postlesson discussion, following a structured agenda (see Figure 5–2) with designated facilitator and note taker.
- Focus discussion on the data collected at the research lesson.
- (Revise lesson and have another team member reteach the revised lesson in another classroom if desired.)

5.	**Reflect and plan the next steps (one to two meetings).**

- Consolidate what you learned (about the subject matter, student thinking, instruction, and other facets). Summarize in a presentation or in writing.
- Discuss what worked well in your lesson study process and what you would like to change next time around.

6.	**Undertaking lesson study is important work to build our profession. Celebrate!**

Figure 3–1 Overall Schedule for One Lesson Study Cycle

Recruit Group Members

Figure 3–2 outlines some strategies for recruiting members of a lesson study group. Perhaps, like Jackie and her colleagues, you find the idea of lesson study appealing and will recruit like-minded colleagues through an open letter to district colleagues. Or maybe you already participate in a group that provides a natural start for lesson study—such as a grade-level group, book group, or subject

STRATEGY	RESOURCES
Build awareness, recruit volunteers.	With colleagues, read an article or book or watch a video on lesson study, in order to identify interested collaborators.
Transform an existing group.	Groups in your district or region may provide a natural start for a lesson study group: • Committees on curriculum, standards, assessment, etc. Research lessons can bring their ideas to life in the classroom, for others to see. • Mentor teachers, coaches, or subject matter specialists. Research lessons provide a way to refine, spread, and examine their ideas about good practice.
Reshape current work to include lesson study.	• Grant-funded work. Perhaps a funder would welcome an open house research lesson instead of the traditional final report. Public research lessons provide built-in accountability and can disseminate grant-funded work. • Professional development credits. Rather than steer teachers toward individual coursework or one-shot conferences, how about making lesson study groups an option? • Program quality review, school improvement plans, etc. Lesson study provides a structure for setting goals, improving instruction, and assessing student development. • Pro forma reviews. Tenured teachers might be given the option of conducting a research lesson in lieu of current requirements (such as observation by the principal).
Contact local members of a union or subject matter organization.	Teachers' unions and subject matter associations have been pioneers of lesson study (e.g., Dubin 2009). Science museums, schools of education, and other local institutions may partner to develop a lesson study group or network.
Find a school with a supportive mission.	An existing or planned magnet school or professional development school could incorporate lesson study as a key operating principle.
Gather your buddies.	Working with a few colleagues, start a small lesson study group, where you can learn together how to do lesson study. If your group builds and shares useful knowledge, interest and support are likely to follow.
Look online.	Information about lesson study groups is beginning to be available online. You may be able to find interested individuals in your area by contacting a lesson study network, e.g., lsnetwork@mailman.depaul.edu.

Figure 3–2 Strategies to Recruit a Lesson Study Group

matter group—that is eager to strengthen its impact on classroom instruction. Successful lesson study efforts can also begin in a summer workshop, where teachers are able to try out lesson study outside the busy pace and demands of the regular school year. Ideally, lesson study should not feel like something additional to do; it should feel like a tool that enables one to work more effectively at the core learning within teaching—for example, learning to use a new curriculum to reach struggling learners, or to enact other current priorities.

Lesson study is most likely to be effective when integrated into other ongoing work, such as implementation of a new curriculum or standards, improvement of instruction in a particular area, long-term planning, or program quality review. Offering lesson study as an alternative way to meet an existing obligation (such as yearly review or professional development credits) recognizes that many teachers need something taken off their plates before they have room for something new. Or perhaps you want to form a group initially with just a few trusted colleagues who also enjoy the challenges of trying an emerging innovation. Whatever approach you choose, remember to be open and welcoming to curious outsiders. A sample first meeting agenda for groups new to lesson study is included in Appendix E to help you get started.

Determining the Best Size and Makeup of Your Group

Optimal group size for planning a research lesson is probably about four to six teachers. But for activities like selecting your research theme, locating good research and curriculum materials, and observing and discussing lessons (particularly on the second or third teaching), you may benefit by working with other groups or invited outsiders.

For school-based lesson study, developing the research theme as a whole faculty provides a very important shared experience for teachers, connecting their work across the school, after which teachers can break into smaller teams to plan research lessons informed by the shared research theme. It is typical for teachers from one grade level or two adjacent grade levels to form a group (since this enables them to focus on a topic at a single or adjacent grade levels). However, groups may be formed in other ways, depending on a school's goals. For example, teachers might form groups based on the particular subject matter they want to research (e.g., writing, mathematics) or the particular differentiation strategy they want to investigate. Cross-grade-level lesson study teams are a powerful way for teachers to understand how a concept develops across the grades. Lower-grade teachers can see the importance of their piece of the curriculum at successive grade levels. Upper-grade teachers can see how younger students learn particular concepts and can connect their own instruction of new concepts to the examples and models used in prior years.

For secondary schools, it is typically most effective to work with teachers who teach in the same content area so that you can build shared ideas about the important concepts, see how the curriculum fits together across years, and work together to deepen your knowledge of recent scholarship and teaching strategies in your shared discipline. However, interdisciplinary lesson study may also work well in certain circumstances. For example, teachers from several disciplines may work together to improve students' writing or their strategies for comprehension of nonfiction. A successful school reform network in Japan includes many junior high schools whose teachers work together across disciplines to build student attendance and connection to school, by reshaping instruction in all subjects to emphasize inquiry and collaboration (Lewis, Akita, and Sato 2010; Sato and Sato 2001). Teachers in different disciplines within a school use shared principles for analysis of instruction, such as whether a lesson elicits the thinking of all students, enables connections between the academic discipline and real-world issues, and so forth. If teachers collaborate across disciplines, it is important that all participants see the lesson study goals as important to their teaching, not as a "side trip" (Sisk-Hilton 2009) or distraction.

Consider an Outside Specialist

Another element that can greatly enhance lesson study is inclusion of an outside specialist, such as a teacher or researcher, who is highly knowledgeable about the subject matter under study, how to teach it, or both. It is often most effective to involve an outside specialist early on, so that the specialist has a chance to contribute ideas about the direction of the work, suggest curricular resources, and schedule time to serve as a commentator on the research lesson. "A Closer Look" highlights the role of the outside specialist in lesson study.

Though not required, an outside specialist may play a crucial role within a school and beyond. If you choose to use an outside specialist, make sure she understands the collaborative, student-focused nature of lesson study. You may want to share Figure 1–1 (page 7) with the specialist, in order to highlight the differences between lesson study and traditional expert-led professional development, and you will certainly want to share the guidelines for observation of a research lesson (Figure 5–1, p. 58). In lesson study, the role of the outside specialist is to raise questions, add new perspectives, and be a co-researcher, not to tell others what to do.

A subject matter specialist (from the district or a university) who meets with the lesson study group can help teachers quickly access relevant research, high-quality curriculum examples, and answers to subject matter questions. A subject matter specialist can greatly ease the work of teachers in pinpointing useful materials within the huge variety of purportedly useful Internet and print resources. However, the regular presence of a subject matter specialist (particularly one who quickly jumps in to help, and whom team members look to as an authority) can also keep teachers from doing certain kinds of learning.

Consider an exchange on the DVD "How Many Seats?" Teachers are anticipating student responses to the seats task, and one teacher suggests that students may arrange the triangle tables incorrectly (not in a row). Another teacher asks whether that will make a difference in the mathematical function that relates the seats and tables. They look to Jackie (who serves half-time as a mathematics coach), who responds, "I wonder if it makes a difference. Let's figure it out." Teachers then try arranging the triangles incorrectly, as they think students might. When some team members are about to conclude prematurely that the pattern always holds, Jackie makes what may be a crucial intervention, asking the question, "Will that always be true?" When subsequently questioned about their experiences during the lesson study cycle, several teachers commented that the experience of posing and solving a novel mathematics problem

A Closer Look: The Role of Outside Specialists in Japanese Lesson Study

by Tad Watanabe, Kennesaw State University

Professor Kenjo is an experienced mathematics teacher educator at a national university known for preservice teacher education. He is often invited to be an outside commentator on research lessons. He says that, as a rule of thumb, he tries to "praise ten and criticize one." In other words, he selects one (or a few) important ideas to focus on and chooses not to dwell on other areas needing improvement. On those issues, he might say something like, "You have done this very well, but perhaps if you think about these ideas, you might be able to do even better." However, on the issue he selects to focus on, he becomes much more critical and provocative.

Professor Kenjo says that when he is invited to be the outside commentator at an open house or research lesson that is more public in nature, he tries to focus on generalizing the main idea of the research lesson. The research lesson is conducted with a particular group of children with a particular teacher. Not everyone can duplicate what the teacher did. However, the outside commentator must, according to Professor Kenjo, generalize the good practices exemplified in the research lesson to assist the observing teachers to think about adopting the practices in their classrooms.

Occasionally, an outside commentator works more closely with a school or a group of teachers. In those situations, the same commentator will attend a number of research lessons conducted by the school or the group over an extended period of time. For example, Professor Saito has been working with Takuma Elementary School, a public elementary school in Tokyo metropolitan area, for more than a year. After a recent lesson study open house, which was attended by more than two hundred teachers from the Tokyo area and beyond, Professor Saito recalled what initial lesson study meetings were like. He said that during his talk, more than half of the faculty was either asleep or pretended to be. However, the principal and Professor Saito, along with the head of the school lesson study group, persisted. Today, all teachers at the school seem to have found joy and excitement in lesson study. During the two years he has been involved, Professor Saito shared his expertise and was also a cheerleader who encouraged the teachers to keep moving on. He even taught a research lesson himself.

As you can see, an outside specialist can play a number of different roles depending on the particular situation. However, one thing that is common to all effective specialists is that they pay attention to the audience and anticipate what they are ready to learn. An experienced teacher recently told me that an outside specialist is just like a teacher in a classroom. Just as a teacher must assess and act according to what students need, the outside commentator must do the same with the teachers who are attending the lesson study.

by themselves—based on a mistake they thought students might make—felt very significant. As one said, "I felt like we were in charge of our own learning." Rather than answering the question, Jackie asked challenging questions that allowed team members to solve the question themselves.

There is no right or wrong answer to the question of whether to include a subject matter specialist. A subject matter specialist may quickly access high-quality resources, substantially enhancing teachers' learning during the cycle. On the other hand, with a subject matter specialist present, teachers may have fewer opportunities to learn how to collect and explore resources, consult research, ask for help, and involve content experts without giving away all power to them. There are many intermediate choices between regular participation by a specialist and no participation. For example, some lesson study groups regularly work with subject matter specialists by email during curriculum study and have them visit as commentators at the time of the research lesson. Another possibility is to have a specialist recommend materials once the group has settled on a topic or to use a "lesson study tool kit" designed to support lesson study on a particular topic. Such tool kits have been developed for several topics in mathematics and include, for example, problems for teachers to solve and discuss, tasks to investigate student thinking, and research summaries. (See toolkit examples for mathematics at: www.lessonresearch.net/nsf_toolkit.html and www.lessonresearch .net/FRACTIONTK/fractions_toolkit.html.)

Develop a Shared Understanding of Lesson Study

However your group comes into being, the work of lesson study is likely to feel like a significant paradigm shift. It is important to create a shared vision for the work you are about to undertake. We suggest that you examine and share your ideas about effective professional development, acquaint yourselves with lesson study, and consider how the two fit together. You can do this by revisiting questions 1 to 3 of the "How Many Seats?" viewing guide in Appendix B.

A Learning Stance

Lesson study rests on the assumption that *everyone* takes a learning stance. It will be helpful for every group member—even ones who are coaches or "experts"—to bring genuine questions (not just answers) to the group's work. Lesson study differs from mentoring or coaching in its emphasis on inquiry conducted by equals, and it provides an opportunity for even experts to pose and pursue questions about student thinking.

Shared Ownership and Responsibility

In their work together, group members should come to feel that the lessons are "our" lessons, not "your" lesson or "my" lesson. The point of lesson study is not to polish the skills of a few star teachers but to help all teachers grow and to create the interpersonal relationships, school culture, and personal and collective habits of inquiry that support continuing growth every day. Members view every participant as having something valuable to contribute to the group.

Emphasis on Students, Not the Teacher

Lesson study focuses on student learning and development. It provides a rare and valuable chance for teachers to be in a classroom solely to investigate student learning, unencumbered by the need to manage students or provide instruction. During a class discussion, a first-year U.S. teacher from Mills College (January 16, 2001) pointed out how lesson study differs from the lesson observation familiar to U.S. teachers: "In the United States, if you are being observed, it's a critique of you. Lesson study focuses on student learning, on student ahas. It takes what we're doing to a more professional level."

Agree on Expectations from Group Members

What contributions will you expect from group members? Some lesson study groups form with the understanding that not all members want to teach a research lesson and that no one will be pressured to do so. Others expect all members will take a turn. It makes sense to discuss these expectations up front.

Another important practical step is to define the work roles needed for productive functioning of your group. Typical roles might include:

- a facilitator, who leads the group through the agenda, eliciting participation from all group members and actively monitoring the group norms
- a note taker, who records and distributes notes that summarize discussions and capture important decisions
- a recorder, who writes on chart paper or the board information that needs to be kept in public view (e.g., the results of a brainstorm or the sequence of steps in a lesson)
- perhaps a timekeeper or a convener, who reminds the group of upcoming meetings and makes arrangements (room, refreshments, etc.)

Once the lesson plan is under development, it may be useful to add a role: updating and circulating the lesson plan. Some groups have also added the roles of "researcher" (tracking down research as needed) and "summarizer." Taking a work role helps team members feel responsible for the learning of other participants as well as their own learning. (This list of lesson study group roles can also be found in Appendix F.)

Permanent or Rotating Facilitator?

Many lesson study groups have team members rotate roles each meeting, a practice that ensures that team members gain experience with different roles. Another alternative is to have a single designated facilitator throughout the lesson study cycle. The strengths and trade-offs of each choice are probably clear: a single designated facilitator (particularly if trained and given time for the job) may become a very helpful "go-to" person for materials, information, and problem solving, helping the group make steady progress. On the other hand, rotating facilitation may build shared responsibility and leadership among all team members and may give quiet members a chance to build their comfort in leadership roles.

When lesson study groups have an appointed facilitator who takes responsibility for keeping the group organized and moving forward, teachers may save time and energy and experience lesson study that feels efficient and productive to all team members. This may be a very good way to begin lesson study. However, teachers can learn to perform all of the roles needed for effective group management, and, in the process, learn important skills that help them work as professionals. Teachers who manage their own lesson study effort (using the rotating roles described in the preceding section) learn, for example, how to set up a timeline and carry out work over an extended time period, how to work with other adults and to listen to their ideas, how to ask for help, how to collect and analyze data, and how to document, synthesize, and present what has been learned. It is no doubt more challenging for teachers to assume all the responsibilities of managing the lesson study cycle—but it also may provide richer opportunities for teachers to develop leadership.

Whether a permanent or rotating facilitator is used, it is worth taking some time to consider what is "good" facilitation. Rebecca Pittard of Volusia County, Florida, in her sixth year of lesson study, says that a good facilitator makes sure everyone feels valued and heard, and lets conversation flow around the key questions and tasks of lesson study, bringing it back only when it strays too far afield.

Develop Group Norms

In some forms of professional development, it is possible to remain anonymous, revealing little about one's own teaching practices, beliefs, or content knowledge. By contrast, lesson study is intimate. Teachers must cross classroom boundaries to take a shared look at student learning and to examine the impact and effectiveness of particular lessons and instructional strategies. As they do so, they must reexamine their own beliefs about teaching and learning. Because lesson study requires teachers to venture beyond their own comfort zone, it is wise to develop group norms that will enable members to learn.

A good way to develop norms is for each member of your group to think about how groups have succeeded or failed in supporting their learning in the past, and then share ideas about the important qualities of a professional learning group. (See Appendix G for a summary of this process.) Teachers in a lesson study group in Fresno, California, searched their individual experiences and came up with the following norms (agreements) for their lesson study work together:

- Listen thoughtfully, with an open mind.
- Share the air.
- Give 100 percent!
- Stay on task.
- Be punctual.
- Have a positive outlook toward self and others.
- Be student-focused always.

Update Group Norms

Development of one's own content knowledge is an obvious part of one's development as a teacher, so it is important to consider norms that will support your academic learning. After several years of lesson study work together, a group of teachers at Willard Middle School in Berkeley, California, added a norm of challenging each other's thinking: "Show respect for each other's ideas . . . yet challenge!" As this example illustrates, norms can be revisited and changed as a group develops; good norms are the ones that continue to improve the work of *your* group, enabling you to support one another's learning. "A Closer Look" reveals the power of choosing one norm (or more) to monitor at each meeting and discussing at the end of the meeting whether it was upheld.

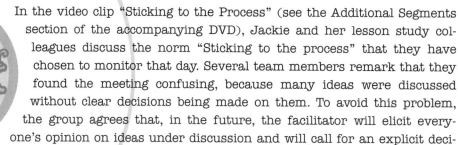

A Closer Look: Sticking to the Process

In the video clip "Sticking to the Process" (see the Additional Segments section of the accompanying DVD), Jackie and her lesson study colleagues discuss the norm "Sticking to the process" that they have chosen to monitor that day. Several team members remark that they found the meeting confusing, because many ideas were discussed without clear decisions being made on them. To avoid this problem, the group agrees that, in the future, the facilitator will elicit everyone's opinion on ideas under discussion and will call for an explicit decision to be made. The final section of the video clip shows the group putting this decision into effect the next day, when the new facilitator asks that group members clarify their decision about one idea before moving on to discussion of the next idea. We think this video clip illustrates how, by monitoring and discussing norms, lesson study groups can hone their processes for working together, creating a more effective set of collaborative practices. When we first embarked on lesson study, some U.S. educators predicted that lesson study could not be practiced outside the collaborative culture of Japan. "Sticking to the process" shows how U.S. educators can *build* a collaborative culture within a lesson study group.

Make a Time Commitment and Set a Schedule

Schools are busy. If you can, schedule times in advance for lesson study meetings for the entire school year so that you are not interrupting the work of each meeting to schedule the next meeting. Creating a schedule for the year also enables you to know when you will need substitutes and, perhaps, outside content specialists. Setting aside lesson study time up front will help protect the natural rhythm of the work even when teachers' lives become hectic. Many U.S. lesson study groups schedule two or three lesson study cycles during the school year, avoiding busy times such as holidays and assessment periods. Advance scheduling is particularly useful in the case of a schoolwide lesson study effort, in which various components, such as a faculty meeting to talk about long-term goals, lesson study team meetings, and research lessons all need to be coordinated. (Figure 3–3 provides a sample one-year schedule.)

How much time does lesson study require?

It may be possible to conduct a lesson study cycle in as little as eight to ten hours, but most groups prefer to spend at least twice that much time. Figure 3–1 (page 30) shows a breakdown of the time within the cycle. If possible, groups should commit up front to do at least two lesson study cycles, because the process usually becomes more comfortable and useful with experience. Two or three lesson study cycles during a school year is typical for a lesson study group.

USING LESSON STUDY TO INVESTIGATE DIFFERENTIATED INSTRUCTION	
Meeting 1	• Develop hypotheses about differentiation: What student needs for differentiation do we currently meet well, and what needs remain? • Select a "dirty" lesson to observe that will provide baseline data on differentiation needs. ("Dirty" lesson means no special planning.) • Identify data you will collect during the lesson to investigate your group's hypotheses about differentiation needs.
Meeting 2	• Discuss information from the district professional development day on differentiation. • Finalize plans for data to be collected during the dirty lesson. Teach, observe, and discuss it before Meeting 3. • Refine the goals for your research lesson based on what you learn about differentiation from the dirty lesson. (Suggest using a half-day sub.)
Meeting 3	• Begin planning the research lesson.
Meeting 4	• Continue planning the research lesson. • Read and discuss any further research or curriculum materials you need to inform your planning.
Meeting 5	• Finalize planning and write-up of the teaching-learning plan for the research lesson. • Teach the research lesson before Meeting 6. • Use a full-day sub for teaching, observing, postlesson discussion, and write-up of what you learned from the lesson.
Meeting 6	• Prepare the results of your research on differentiated instruction to share with the staff.
Meeting 7	• Hold a staff meeting to share out the results from all of the lesson study groups. • This plan utilizes only one and a half of the sub days. You will still have a half of a sub day for observing another research lesson.

Figure 3-3 Sample Plan for Schoolwide Lesson Study

During or After School?

Lesson study meetings can take place either during or after school hours. Because the research lesson itself includes students, it generally takes place during school hours and requires the observing teachers to be released from their own teaching responsibilities for the period of the lesson. (Some schools arrange in advance for one class to stay after school.) Another way to free up one class for a research lesson is to integrate your lesson study plan with a scheduled ongoing schoolwide activity (such as an art or literacy project, community service project, or science fair) that students participate in regularly over the course of a year, with just the students from the research lesson class missing this activity on a rotating basis. Often such activities can include parent and community volunteers, specialist teachers from outside the school, artists in residence, or other adults who can free up classroom teachers while providing a vital learning experience for children. Books like *At Home in Our Schools* (Developmental Studies Center 1994) provide suggestions for such schoolwide events.

Meetings that include just teachers from one or two grade levels may be scheduled during a common planning time or at a time when the principal or assistant principal can teach these classes. This can be a wonderful opportunity for school or district administrators to demonstrate their commitment to teachers' professional development and retaste the flavor of classroom life!

In "A Closer Look," principal Lynn Liptak notes that scheduling of lesson study depends upon making clever use of the existing resources, such as non-classroom teachers, support services, departmentalization, student lunch time, administrators, and so forth. The guiding principles behind scheduling are to maintain high-quality instruction for students and to schedule lesson study in a way that will permit it to become part of school culture.

In contrast to Paterson School No. 2, the San Mateo lesson study groups initially met after school, but they conducted research lessons during school hours, using substitute teachers to cover the classes of planning team members who were observing the lesson. Over the course of their work, many San Mateo groups found ways to integrate group meeting times into the school day, by re-purposing staff meeting time and using district-mandated professional development days. For after-school meetings, a modest stipend was provided from grant funding from sources that varied over the years, including district funds targeted for math and science professional development and grants from private foundations. (Foundation funding also included support from The Noyce Foundation for teacher-coaches in mathematics and small grants from the Spencer Foundation and Kabcenell Foundation.)

Optimal Time Between Meetings

An optimal schedule includes weekly meetings for a ten- to fourteen-week lesson study cycle, with two or three lesson study cycles during the year and breaks from lesson study at busy times of year. Within each lesson study cycle, it is optimal to revise and reteach the research lesson at least once if feasible. However, we have seen successful lesson study efforts that use meetings spaced two to four weeks apart (good note taking and distribution are essential to allow members to remind themselves quickly about what went on at the prior meeting) or that have

A Closer Look: Scheduling Lesson Study in an American School

by Lynn Liptak, Principal, Paterson School No. 2, Paterson, New Jersey

The following principles were considered in developing a lesson study schedule for School Number 2, Paterson, NJ:

- If lesson study is going to become part of the school culture and conducted over a long period with a goal of gradual improvement, then time must be allocated during the school day. Lesson study has no chance of becoming a prevalent feature of the school culture if it is conducted with a few enthusiastic volunteers working after school.

- Time is one sure measure of commitment. When teachers see serious time committed to lesson study, and the administrators taking time to engage in lesson study, they feel confident of a high level of support for the process on a day-to-day basis and over the long haul.

- Lesson study should be scheduled by reallocating currently existing resources. In our school, it does not rely on "soft" money or the hiring of substitute teachers.

- Quality instruction must be provided in the classroom while the teachers are engaged in lesson study.

Time for lesson study is thus built into the regular school day using non-classroom teachers and preservice teachers. Each classroom teacher is paired with a nonclassroom partner teacher. The partner teacher has contact with the class during the week by teaching during teacher preparation periods, downsizing the class for mathematics or reading, or tutoring individual students. It is the responsibility of the partner teacher to know the students and become familiar with classroom routines. In the event of absence, the partner teacher helps to orient the substitute and assist, as needed, with the class. The partner teacher often teaches the class while the classroom teacher engages in lesson study.

During the first cycle of lesson study, it was apparent that the two-hour weekly meeting was only "seed" time. Once we began to collaborate on lessons and test out ideas in the classroom, we did not wait until Monday to continue the process. Email communication and discussions before and after school, during lunch periods and preparation periods are common. Most important, these discussions and observations are focused on how our teaching impacts student learning. We know from research and our own observations that grade-level meetings and school management team meetings rarely focus on the lessons that occur daily in the classrooms.

For too long, in my view, professional development time in the United States has been allocated to outside experts to "train" teachers, rather than given to educators to reflect collaboratively on their practice. We need to tap outside expertise; we need to improve our content and pedagogical knowledge. But the professional development process needs to occur in the context of our classrooms and be driven by professional practitioners. Lesson study—it's about time.

met intensively over two to five days of whole-day meetings (for example, during a summer workshop or grouped professional development days). Bill Jackson, an experienced U.S. lesson study practitioner (Lewis 2002, p. 48) gives the following advice about scheduling lesson study:

> It is important for teachers to understand that lesson study has a definite beginning and ending. Too much time spent in a cycle can be counterproductive. . . . Teachers should understand that since lesson study is not about making a perfect lesson, a semirigid schedule is needed.

Scheduling research lessons in advance for particular dates during the year—rather than waiting until you feel completely "ready"—can speed up your progress, much the way a deadline can catalyze work on other projects. Likewise, scheduling in advance the second teaching of the lesson can streamline the lesson revision process. The research lesson needs to be discussed soon after it is held (preferably on the same day). Intervals between other lesson study events need to be given some thought. In Japan, reteaching generally occurs soon after the original lesson (within a few days or a week), and some U.S. schools follow this practice. Other U.S. schools choose a longer interval (for example, two to three weeks) before reteaching. Bill Jackson, formerly a teacher and mathematics coach at Paterson Public School No. 2, noted that teaching the lesson the first time often highlights gaps in students' prior knowledge, enabling the lesson study group to identify basic concepts to be firmed up in lessons taught before the teaching of the revised lesson. Like the teachers at Paterson Public School No. 2, you will want to adjust your second lesson study cycle to reflect what you learn the first time around. The sooner you do an actual research lesson, the sooner you will be able to learn from the process.

A sample timeline from Highlands School (Appendix H) illustrates the power of setting a timeline for the whole lesson study cycle. Additionally, the meeting protocol that was established by Highlands teachers to help their groups function efficiently and stay on course is included in Appendix I. Alice Gill, director of mathematics professional development for the American Federation of Teachers, recommends that you set a date for the research lesson and stick to it, even if you don't feel ready. She notes that we can never be perfectly ready and that observing students in action provides a valuable stimulus for insights into student thinking, which become the basis for continued improvement of teaching.

chapter 4

Focus the Group's Inquiry

The opportunity to focus on two to four students' learning was incredible. . . . You feel like you are in a true research mode.

—ELEMENTARY TEACHER, AFTER LESSON STUDY CYCLE

Develop a Research Theme

To focus your lesson study, we suggest that you first develop a research theme that captures your long-term goals for students. (If your lesson study group is part of larger schoolwide or organizational work, it is good to develop the research theme collectively with other lesson study groups.) The research theme is usually a broad goal that is compelling to teachers from all grade levels and many points of view, such as to build student' desire to learn, responsibility and initiative as learners, and habits of learning and inquiry. The lesson study cycle "How Many Seats?" occurred during a summer mathematics institute focused on the research theme of developing students' algebraic reasoning skills. The lesson study team involved in the cycle "Improving Student Writing" addressed the schoolwide research theme of exploring effective differentiation strategies to support underperforming students.

Two questions should shape the research theme:

- Ideally, what qualities will students have when they graduate from our school?
- What are the actual qualities of our students now?

One teacher defined lesson study as follows: "The students' actual situation right now is the starting point for your journey and students' ideal qualities are your destination. Lesson study is the road that links the two" (Yukinobu Okada, comments at Greenwich Japanese School Open House, November 13, 2000). By comparing the "ideal" and "actual" qualities of students, you can locate the most meaningful focus for your group's lesson study. Appendix J provides a guide to develop the research theme.

As you develop your research theme, you may also want to consider important local mandates and to integrate these into your thinking about long-term goals. For example, Highlands School focused in successive years on district mandates including standards-based instruction and differentiated instruction. In the case of standards-based instruction, each group chose a standard to focus on in their lesson study work; in the case of differentiated instruction, the whole school read a book on differentiation strategies, and each group chose a strategy to study, bring to life, and investigate in their lesson study work.

As you develop the research theme, it is also a good time to think about your own personal learning goals: What would you like to learn about students, about subject matter, or about your own teaching? In some settings, each member of a lesson study group chooses an individual inquiry question, in addition to the questions investigated by the group as a whole. For example, teachers in the history–social studies lesson study groups in Oakland Unified School District (California) formulate individual inquiry questions such as "How do students use primary source materials?" or "What connections do students notice between [a given historical event] and contemporary events?" Likewise, many districts in Japan provide special lesson study opportunities for all teachers in their fifth (tenth, fifteenth) year of teaching, and each teacher develops an inquiry question related to his own teaching and uses lesson study to investigate it, with other teachers in the cohort serving as observers. Teachers at a similar point in their careers often find one another's inquiry questions very relevant to their own challenges and questions related to teaching.

One lesson study team took on investigation of the question "How do we build just right, engaging activities for students of all readiness levels to participate in during readers' workshop?" The lesson study team consisted of a district literacy coach, a school reading recovery teacher, two first-grade teachers, and a second-grade teacher. Because the team consisted of professionals with differing lenses, each participant also posed a secondary research question more specific to her individual interests and challenges.

Choose a Topic

As you turn your attention to choosing the subject area of your lesson study work, your group may want to think about the following questions:

- What topics are persistently difficult for, or disliked by, students?

- What topics do teachers find most difficult to teach?

- In what subjects are there new curricula, frameworks, or standards that teachers want to understand and master?

Student work, performance assessments, and test data may also be helpful in narrowing the focus of your lesson study work.

As you home in on a specific topic for your lesson study, it may be useful to revisit your long-term goals for students in light of particular students or groups of students in your classes. Call to mind the individual faces and needs of your students, consider the challenges you face in the classroom, and think about the topics that are fundamental to students' future learning. Alternately, you may simply choose whatever topic happens to be taught at the time of the scheduled research lesson, with the idea that all lessons should provide a window on your long-term goals and students' approaches to the discipline of history, mathematics, writing, or whatever the focus of your work.

The task of choosing a unit and lesson for the focus of lesson study can be very easy or very difficult. Some lesson study groups report that diagnostic tests clearly identify a problem (for example, student difficulty with word problems) but may not provide a clear idea about the kinds of instruction that would better develop student understanding. One lesson study group originally thought their students were having difficulty with the place value of ones and tens, but as they began to design a lesson, they found that the real problem seemed to be students' fluency with addition and subtraction to twenty. Another group ultimately changed their lesson topic after several meetings. "It takes time coming to one mind. You fumble along the way. You spend time going down dead ends. At our third meeting, we realized we were wrestling with a topic we didn't care enough about. You have to be patient with the process" (Mary Pat O'Connell, personal communication, January 16, 2002).

Some lesson study groups begin by teaching a lesson that is not as carefully crafted as a research lesson but enables the teachers to gain information about student thinking that can be used to plan the research lesson. Teachers might choose a lesson that they commonly teach each year on the topic of interest. One teacher teaches the lesson while others observe and collect data on student thinking. We casually referred to this as a "dirty" lesson because we spent little time on planning at this point. The purpose of this preliminary lesson is to reveal students' strengths and areas of need. One lesson study group working on sound patterns in spelling taught a dirty lesson drawn from a popular curriculum, and they noticed that students' weak understanding of prefixes and suffixes hindered their recognition of sound patterns. This discovery altered the direction of their lesson study work.

Another way to provide data for lesson planning is for group members to choose a task related to their topic of focus, give it to their students, and bring the student work back to the lesson study group for discussion. Teachers in one school we know put the lesson task up in the teachers' room on a large poster and ask their fellow teachers to share anticipated student responses, as a way of getting ideas from colleagues outside the lesson study group.

Avoid "Side Trip" Lessons

Sometimes a lesson study group ends up choosing a research lesson that is not central to their curriculum or teaching. For example, teachers may decide to focus on a "fun" lesson that is not really important to anyone's curriculum. Or teachers from different disciplines collaborating in interdisciplinary lesson study may look for a lesson that they can all teach and end up with a compromise lesson that does not really feel important to any of them. Privatization of teaching within a school may lead teachers to focus on a topic that is safely outside what they usually teach (Sisk-Hilton 2009). If you feel like your lesson study group is headed toward a "side trip" lesson, check in with group members and try to reorient. Even if the specific topic of the lesson is not one that could be taught by each member, it should be an important part of the curriculum for some member of the group, and there should be elements that interest all group members. Such elements might be teaching-learning strategies relevant to all team members—such as how to elicit student thinking, how to help students organize and present their thinking, how to discuss and compare ideas, or how to use journals or the blackboard to help students consolidate and advance their thinking.

Study Standards, Curriculum, and Research

Planning a research lesson takes more time than planning a regular daily lesson. (That's why most lesson study groups do just two or three lesson study cycles per year.) The point of the lesson study cycle is not simply to produce a lesson, but to study the topic and student thinking in some depth.

Lesson study is most productive when educators build on the best existing lessons and research, rather than reinventing the wheel. Try to immerse yourself in good lessons through whatever means you can (observation of colleagues, videos, etc.) and to study curriculum and research related to the topic of your lesson. Lesson study is most satisfying and productive when all team members learn something. Alice Gill, who facilitates a network of mathematics lesson study groups across the United States, notes, "If we work just in our own heads and with familiar textbooks, we won't get anything new." Knowledge and perspectives from outside the group—in the form of research studies, high-quality curriculum, regional or university-based content specialists, and so forth—may greatly enrich a team's learning. Lesson study creates the dedicated time and collegial support for careful review of materials from the teacher's manual and other resources designed to support teachers' learning. To deepen knowledge of the topic under study, it will be useful for your lesson study group to:

- Carefully study your own curriculum, especially any supporting materials in the teacher's manual designed to build in-depth content knowledge.

- Compare your curriculum with a different curriculum (perhaps one that is strongly research-based, is recommended by a national subject matter organization, or is from a foreign country), in order to find contrasting approaches and ideas that illuminate how students learn this particular content. Some tested toolkits of useful materials to support mathematics lesson study can be found at www.lessonresearch.net/nsf_toolkit.html and www.lesson research.net/FRACTIONTK/fractions_toolkit.html.

- Consult knowledgeable outsiders, such as district, regional, or university-based coaches and subject matter specialists. By searching out local specialists and subject matter networks, groups may be able to access outside expertise without great difficulty or expense. For example, lesson study groups working with the "Thinking Mathematics" network supported by American Federation of Teachers' Alice Gill regularly use email to get university-based mathematics educators to react to their emerging ideas and lesson plans.

- Acquaint yourself with research on the topic under study—for example, research on student conceptions, or recent advances in knowledge. Knowledgeable outsiders and websites of subject matter associations can both be excellent sources of such information.

Select some materials to collectively read and discuss (or, in the case of video, to watch). Share your thinking—and the thinking of those who have gone before you—to help build a collective background for development of the research lesson. Much is learned as teachers share their collective wisdom. But it is also important to advance the collective wisdom, by going beyond the group to become familiar with existing curriculum materials and research.

The following questions may help guide your study of curriculum and research:

- What are the important understandings students need to develop about this topic, and how do they develop?

- How do different curricula treat this topic, and what are the advantages and disadvantages of each? What might be the impact of the models, examples, or approaches used by different curricula?

- What does research tell us about student understanding and how it develops?

If your group searches out and studies the best existing lessons, it will produce a high-quality research lesson and help create a system that learns. As Isaac Newton reflected on the cumulative progress of science in a letter dated February 5, 1676, "If I have seen further . . . it is by standing on the shoulders of giants." In the United States, we have an abundance of educational research, curriculum resources, and pedagogical guides. Lesson study creates the time, space, and *need* to carefully examine these materials in order to improve teaching of a particular topic.

Develop a Teaching-Learning Plan

After you have chosen your research theme and explored the curriculum and materials on your topic, you are ready to begin constructing the teaching-learning plan. The teaching-learning plan guides the teaching, observation, and discussion of the research lesson, and captures the inquiry that occurs in your lesson study group. The teaching-learning plan differs from an ordinary lesson plan because it is designed to stimulate, capture, and share your learning, as well as guide the lesson.

The teaching-learning plan represents the thinking of your lesson study group at three layers of practice: the lesson itself, the larger unit and subject area of which it is part, and the even larger domain of students' long-term development. As you move from planning to doing the research lesson, the teaching-learning plan will:

- support the research lesson instructor, by providing a detailed outline of the lesson and its logistical details (such as time, materials, and wording of key questions or problems)

- guide data collection, by specifying "points to notice" and providing appropriate data collection forms

- help observers understand the lesson (by providing an overview and copies of student worksheets) and the lesson rationale, including reasons for particular pedagogical choices and their connection to long-term goals

- record the group's thinking and planning to date, so that you can later revisit these and share them with others

The teaching-learning plan can help your team members think through the research lesson itself as well as the larger unit. A Japanese teacher writes that the teaching-learning plan is:

> a hypothesis for the lesson. . . . The teaching-learning plan needs to express the problem that necessitated this lesson, what the lesson newly proposes, and it must include the teacher's own vision of education, of children, of mathematics. . . . It's a great deal of work. But through writing it, you become aware of how you think about lessons and about content. (Ishikawa et al. 2001)

It may be helpful to think about the elements of the teaching-learning plan in three concentric circles, with the research lesson plan at the center, the unit plan in the next ring out, and the whole teaching-learning plan as the outermost ring, as illustrated in Figure 4–1.

Your process may not proceed in exactly the order described here. For example, you may consult an outside specialist as part of your teaching-learning plan development, or you may revise your teaching-learning plan after trying it in practice. Because the teaching-learning plan plays several important roles and yet may be unfamiliar, your group might want to carefully analyze the teaching-learning plan in Appendix K. It provides a good window on the planning that leads up to the research lesson and a framework for your own teaching-learning plan (which can be created using the template in Appendix L). Note each element in the plan and allot time to discuss each, including the lesson and unit goals, learning flow of the entire unit, detailed lesson plan, and so forth.

Outer Circle: The Research Theme

When you developed the research theme, you considered the qualities you would like students to have in the future. Remind yourself of these qualities, and consider how the lesson you are about to plan will help you develop those qualities. Planners of the "How Many Seats?" lesson wanted students to develop their algebraic reasoning and become curious about mathematical patterns. In your

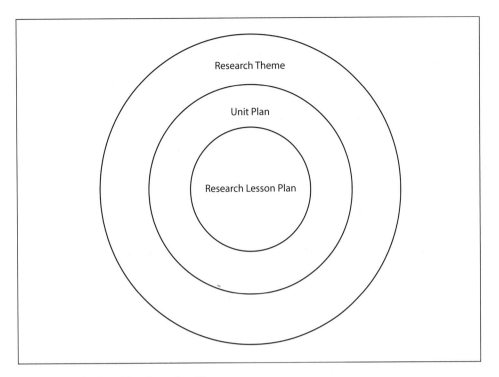

Figure 4-1 The Teaching-Learning Plan

teaching-learning plan, you may want to include comments or a map like that shown in Figure 4–2 that connects your research lesson to your long-term goals for students. For example, you might outline your hypotheses about the experiences that nurture mathematical curiosity in students. Appendix M provides a blank research map.

Second Circle: The Unit Plan

Although U.S. educators often think of lesson study as focusing on a single lesson; in fact, it focuses on the whole unit, even though just one lesson is typically observed. The unit plan shows how the observed research lesson fits into a series of lessons. For example, when Akihiko Takahashi taught a series of lessons on area of polygons to fourth graders in San Mateo, California, each lesson successively laid the groundwork for students to transform unfamiliar shapes (such as parallelograms) into familiar shapes (such as rectangles) in order to find the area. Although the eventual goal of the entire unit was for students to construct the formula for area of a parallelogram, the goal of each lesson was more modest. (The lesson plans are available at: www.lessonresearch.net/AreaGeoboard _4thgrade.pdf.)

From reading the unit plan within the teaching-learning plan, lesson observers can see the entire flow of the unit and can tell, for example, whether the primary function of the lesson is to motivate students to study the topic in subsequent lessons, to help students learn a new concept, or to help students consolidate and apply what they have learned in prior lessons. The teaching-learning

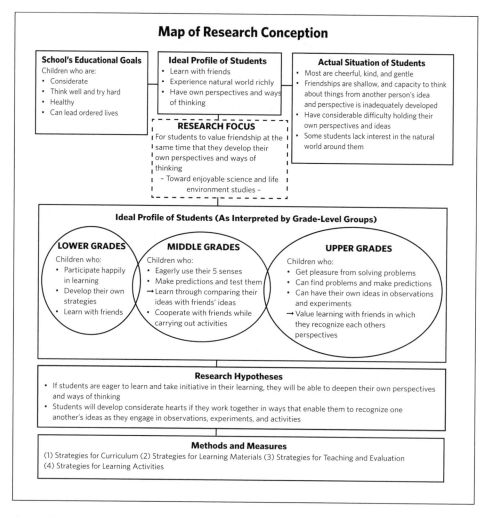

Map of Research Conception

School's Educational Goals
Children who are:
- Considerate
- Think well and try hard
- Healthy
- Can lead ordered lives

Ideal Profile of Students
- Learn with friends
- Experience natural world richly
- Have own perspectives and ways of thinking

Actual Situation of Students
- Most are cheerful, kind, and gentle
- Friendships are shallow, and capacity to think about things from another person's idea and perspective is inadequately developed
- Have considerable difficulty holding their own perspectives and ideas
- Some students lack interest in the natural world around them

RESEARCH FOCUS
For students to value friendship at the same time that they develop their own perspectives and ways of thinking
– Toward enjoyable science and life environment studies –

Ideal Profile of Students (As Interpreted by Grade-Level Groups)

LOWER GRADES
Children who:
- Participate happily in learning
- Develop their own strategies
- Learn with friends

MIDDLE GRADES
Children who:
- Eagerly use their 5 senses
- Make predictions and test them
→ Learn through comparing their ideas with friends' ideas
- Cooperate with friends while carrying out activities

UPPER GRADES
Children who:
- Get pleasure from solving problems
- Can find problems and make predictions
- Can have their own ideas in observations and experiments
→ Value learning with friends in which they recognize each others perspectives

Research Hypotheses
- If students are eager to learn and take initiative in their learning, they will be able to deepen their own perspectives and ways of thinking
- Students will develop considerate hearts if they work together in ways that enable them to recognize one another's ideas as they engage in observations, experiments, and activities

Methods and Measures
(1) Strategies for Curriculum (2) Strategies for Learning Materials (3) Strategies for Teaching and Evaluation (4) Strategies for Learning Activities

Figure 4-2 Sample Map of Research Conception

plan may also show how the research lesson topic connects with material taught in prior or subsequent years of schooling (see the plan provided in Appendix K). Another example of unit objectives and a unit teaching-learning plan can be found in the plan for "Can You Lift 100 Kilograms?" found in Appendix N.

The Innermost Core: The Research Lesson Plan

Located near the middle or end of the teaching-learning plan is a detailed plan for the research lesson itself, often called "today's lesson" or "the progression of the [research] lesson." (See Section 8 of the teaching-learning plan found in Appendix K.) The research lesson plan answers the central question: What changes in student thinking will occur during the lesson, and what will provoke them? This research lesson plan is usually written out in three or four parallel columns that contain:

- the questions, problems, and activities to be posed by the teacher, and the time allocated for each
- the anticipated student responses

- the teacher's planned responses to the students and things for the teacher to remember
- points to notice during the lesson (or "evaluation") (This alerts observers about what to look for at each stage of the lesson. For example, observers might be cued to notice what methods students use to investigate a problem introduced by the teacher, what types of conjectures they make from primary source photographs, or how their drawings of hot air change after conducting an experiment.)

The following list of questions may be helpful as you develop the research lesson plan:

1. What do students currently understand about this topic? (The lesson rationale captures this information.)

2. What do we want students to understand at the end of the lesson? (The goals of the plan capture this.)

3. What is the "drama," or sequence of questions and experiences that will propel students from their initial understanding to the desired understanding? (This information is recorded in the first column of the Research Lesson Plan, Student Learning Activities.)

4. How will students respond to the questions and activities in the lesson? What kinds of thinking, problems, and misconceptions will arise, and how will the teacher use these ideas and misconceptions to advance the lesson? (This information is recorded in the second column, Anticipated Student Responses and Teacher Response.)

5. What will make this lesson motivating and meaningful to students? (This information is recorded under Lesson Rationale.)

6. What evidence should we gather and discuss about student learning, motivation, and behavior? (This information is recorded under Points to Notice within the Research Lesson Plan.)

7. What data collection forms are needed to do this? (Data collection forms are provided at the end of the Teaching-Learning Plan.)

Addressing the preceding questions will help you formulate your goals for the research lesson. You will probably find that you have two types of goals for the lesson—goals for teachers and goals for students. For example, as teachers you may be interested in research questions like:

- What different strategies do students invent to add fractions with unlike denominators, and what do these strategies reveal about students' understanding of fractions?
- How do students refine their story outlines after dramatizing them to a friend?
- What historical information do students bring to bear on interpretation of primary texts?

You will also have goals for student learning during the lesson, as described earlier—for example, for students to learn a particular strategy to revise writing, or to discover and represent mathematically the patterns in a problem. These goals for students occur at the following four levels of breadth.

Identify Goals

Once you've chosen a topic, you will want to study the goals or standards for that topic specified in your district, state, or other relevant content materials. With these in mind, you can sketch out a series of lessons, one or more of which (the research lessons) you plan in detail. For example, in the video "Can You Lift 100 Kilograms?" the unit goals (achieved over nine lessons) are for students to learn three principles of levers and understand the lever's parts. The goal of the research lesson is for students to discover how hard it is to lift a heavy object by hand, so that they will actively consider ways to ease lifting. Discovering how hard it is to lift a heavy object by hand, the plan explains, will set the stage for students to actively pursue "as their own problem" the three principles of levers that are to be learned during the remaining seven lessons of the unit. Figure 4–3 provides further examples of goals at each of the four levels from the two lesson study cycles described in Chapter Two; they will become clearer as your group develops its teaching-learning plan.

Build Opportunities to Observe Student Thinking

Design your research lesson so that observers will have as many windows as possible into student thinking. If students are working independently on worksheets that do not reveal their thinking and they are not asked to explain their thinking, observers may feel frustrated. A lesson that asks students to work on thought-revealing tasks, to justify their ideas to partners, to explain their thinking in whole-class discussion, to turn and talk to classmates, or to write about what they learned will provide more chances to gather data on student thinking and discourse.

HOW MANY SEATS?	IMPROVING STUDENT WRITING
Level 1 Goals Specific to the Lesson	
Students will discover and describe a mathematical pattern.	Students will experiment with adding emotion to a notebook entry.
Level 2 Goals Specific to the Unit	
Students will understand that patterns can be expressed as mathematical rules.	Students will use strategies for adding emotion to writing, and will see the value of these strategies to pull readers into their writing.
Level 3 Broad Subject Matter Goals	
Students will be able to represent their thinking with numbers and symbols.	Students will actively use a variety of strategies to improve their own writing and peers' writing, improving their use of the strategies over time.
Level 4 Long-Term Goals for Student Development	
Students will be curious learners, interested in exploring new topics.	Students will demonstrate perseverance in their learning.

Figure 4–3 Four Levels of Lesson Study Goals: Examples from the Two Lessons

Avoid Micromanaging the Lesson

As you plan the research lesson, group members may be tempted to micromanage each move and comment of the lesson instructor. Teacher moves are what we know best, and it may be more comfortable to plan teacher moves than to deeply explore the disciplinary content. However, studying the content and curriculum may yield implications for teaching more naturally. If a lesson element is likely to affect students' learning in important ways, then it is probably legitimate territory for group discussion. Problem wording and content, choice of manipulatives, and design of graphic organizers are all examples of lesson elements that may affect student learning. On the other hand, decisions such as whether to have a discussion at desks or gathered on the rug may best be left to the instructor, unless these relate to student learning—for example, if it is important to be at desks so that students can record their thinking in notebooks.

Anticipate Student Thinking

Teacher Heather Crawford notes that planning of a research lesson focuses on student thinking, and that it is initially difficult to move beyond a focus on teacher moves:

> It is challenging—to try to think about the students' solutions to the problem before they do it, and to try to get all of the answers they might come up with. You have to think about things from the student's point of view, and that is a big change. . . . Before we did lesson study, we really didn't think about what the student responses would be to the questions. When we posed a problem, we never really thought about what the kids would come up with. It was, "Well, we hope they get the right answer and if they don't then we will deal with it." Now we are really thinking about, "Well, what if this answer were to come up? How would we deal with it?". . . [Now] we think a lot more about the motivation for the lesson and making sure that the kids have the prior knowledge that they need before we teach each lesson.

Kazuyoshi Morita writes that he builds the research lesson plan by imagining "If I say this, what are the children likely to say?" He goes on to say that "the ability to imagine such a simulation is one strength of a good teacher" (Lewis 2002, p. 65).

Novice lesson study groups sometimes find it hard to anticipate student thinking. The following experiences may help your group anticipate student thinking.

1. *Try the lesson task yourselves.* It is useful for each member of your team to solve the problem or try the task(s) you're considering for the lesson (as if you were students) and to share your responses, using your own and colleagues' solutions to expand your thinking about possible student responses. You may also want to try a task similar to that in the lesson but more challenging to adults, so that you can experience some struggle, as your students will. Another variant that may be useful is "microteaching" in which one member of your group teaches the lesson to the other group members, who serve as students. In any of these activities, be sure to save time to discuss different responses that did (or did

not) arise and to notice and discuss any responses that are unexpected or offer insights into the subject matter and how it is learned.

One Japanese teacher describes how he first "tests" his research lesson plan on an imaginary audience of children:

> Something that you often hear said is "The research lesson was constrained by the lesson plan, so it didn't go well." I think we teachers must do a lesson twice. The first time is with imaginary students as partners, and the second time is with the actual students of the classroom as partners. When you feel constrained by the lesson plan, it's because the first lesson with imaginary students failed. If you put your hopes into a lesson that is based only on your thinking, without considering the ideas it will elicit from students, you will face a painful gap with reality. (Ishikawa et al. 2001, p. 18)

2. *Have each group member try the lesson task (or a related task) with their students and bring back student responses to the group.* Student work or video of clinical interviews with students can be a powerful way of expanding your knowledge of student thinking. Teachers in Sonoma, California, captured video of students solving mathematics problems and discussing their solutions and thinking with teacher-interviewers. These mathematics clinical interviews have provided a powerful catalyst for Sonoma educators to discuss how students approach key mathematical topics (SCOE 2009).

3. *Ask knowledgeable others and consult research and curriculum materials to find out what is known about student thinking and development related to your lesson topic.* Experienced teachers, coaches, and researchers can often provide much information on what students find difficult with respect to particular topics, as well as insight into the experiences that may help students move along a trajectory of understanding. Teachers' manuals, research articles, and curriculum materials may also be good sources of information. For example, Japanese elementary mathematics textbooks typically provide several different students' solution methods for each problem (Hironaka and Sugiyama 2006). The study of teaching materials is an important part of lesson study in Japan, and one that has enabled Japanese teachers to build an extensive, shared knowledge base about student thinking.

Anticipation of student thinking will help with many facets of lesson study work. It will help you develop a compelling design for your lesson, as you think through how you are going to help students build upon their current thinking. It will help you think through, ahead of time, the ideas students may share during the lesson and how to respond to those ideas in the heat of classroom action. It may also help you notice student thinking during the lesson. For example, during their curriculum study, one lesson study group read a research summary on elementary school students' understanding of area that pointed out that students initially find it difficult to systematically divide up the space within a rectangle and that students using squares to measure a space by "covering" it may overlap the squares or leave gaps between them (Driscoll et al. 2007). Several team members were surprised to see students actually do this during the lesson and wondered out loud if reading about this aspect of student thinking had enabled them to see it in the swift movement of classroom events. (Appendix O provides a guide that will help your group anticipate student responses.)

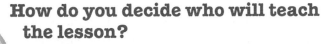

How do you decide who will teach the lesson?

In some lesson study groups, each member agrees to teach a research lesson during the year; this is particularly easy to do if teachers within a lesson study group teach the same curriculum and it is possible to teach successive revisions of the lesson in several different team members' classrooms. Often the person(s) to teach the lesson naturally emerges in the planning process. For example, one member of the group may have a strong vision for the lesson and interest in seeing the lesson with their own students. We know of some lesson study groups that plan the lesson without knowing who will teach it, and then select the instructor's name from a hat near the end of the planning process. There are downsides to this strategy, such as the need for a lesson that will work in any classroom, but it can be a good starting point for building a feeling of "We're all in it together." In Japan, many schools expect every teacher to teach at least one research lesson a year.

Design a Data Collection Plan

The data collection plan focuses your observation of the lesson. What data will tell you how students are grappling with the major ideas of the lesson? Well-designed data collection during the lesson supports a rich postlesson discussion. Members of the lesson study group usually have specific data collection assignments and forms to support data collection, which might include one or more of the following:

- a seating chart
- a list of members of each student group
- records of students' prior thinking
- checklists to note features of student work, such as solution strategies or ideas students might come up with
- forms to record the participation of each member of a small group
- forms to record verbatim the speech and actions of selected students

Other lesson observers (from the school or outside) may also be given data collection assignments or suggestions. Although lesson study novices are often tempted to roam the classroom and see what every student is doing during the research lesson, it is more fruitful if most team members follow selected students or small groups over the entire lesson, in order to see the moment the lightbulb goes on (or doesn't) and to understand the key supports or barriers to the learning of the observed students. You may want to designate one team member to gather data across the class (for example, how many students used each type of solution) if you cannot obtain this information from student work.

Design of data collection is a crucial and difficult part of lesson study. Data collected need to reflect your research questions and specific lesson goals. You will want to collect data on students from groups important to your work (for example, second-language learners and native speakers or reluctant and eager writers). Asking one team member to keep a running record of the teacher's actions and speech and major student reactions (with notations of time) can also provide a valuable overall record of the lesson that reveals how much time was devoted to each phase of the lesson. As you become comfortable with lesson study, a verbatim record of the teacher's speech can be very interesting. (It is probably best for your group to establish a focus on student thinking and a strong lesson study culture before adding a focus on the teacher's speech.)

The data collected by the observers will enable you to slow down the "swiftly flowing river" of instruction in order to study it. Document the research lesson in as many ways as you can conveniently manage—for example, audiotape, videotape, still photography, student work, and narrative observation notes. If you can assign two or more teachers to collect data on a particular child or group of children, you create a natural opportunity for teachers to learn about the strengths and shortcomings of their own observational skills. For example, one teacher we know says she learned to notice children's nonverbal behavior after comparing her own observational notes with those of another teacher and realizing that she tended to miss nonverbal cues. (A data collection guide can be found in Appendix P.)

Write the Lesson Rationale

Although the rationale for the lesson is typically provided at the beginning of the lesson plan, it is often written (or rewritten) last. Notes from all of your group meetings will come in very handy here, to explain decisions your group made about lesson structure based on your discussions, experiences, and examination of research. The lesson rationale helps the reader understand the journey that led you to this lesson and answers questions such as:

- Why did we choose to focus on this topic?

- Why did we design the unit and lesson as we did?

- What student work, student data, teaching experiences, and research shaped our thinking about lesson and unit design?

- What do we think will happen and what do we hope to find out?

Conduct and Discuss the Research Lesson

What's the most important benefit of lesson study? You develop the eyes to see children.

—KYOICHI ITOH, ELEMENTARY PRINCIPAL, NAGOYA, JAPAN

The real voyage of discovery lies not in seeking new landscapes but in having new eyes.

—MARCEL PROUST (1871–1922)

Preparing for the Lesson Observation

By the day of the research lesson, your group will have developed a teaching-learning plan that:

- captures your best collective thinking about how to teach this particular topic to these students
- explains your long-term goals for students and how you will bring them to life in the classroom

- lays out the activities to be posed by the teacher and anticipates the responses of students

- anticipates problems that may occur and how they will be handled (for example, how to support students who can't get started writing, how calculation errors will be handled)

- lists practical information, such as the materials needed for the lesson and how much time will be allocated to each part of the lesson

- tells observers what to look for during each part of the lesson and what data to collect, and provides needed forms (for example, a student seating chart, prior work from each "focus child" of interest, or note-taking forms specifically designed to collect data of interest)

Now it's time for the most interesting part of any research effort—seeing how your ideas fare in practice. Figure 5–1 provides lesson observation guidelines; they deserve careful review by each member of your team and each observer of the research lesson. The role of the observers during lesson study is to collect data. As U.S. researchers have noted, the observers are supposed to function as "an extra set of eyes, not an extra set of hands" (Fernandez, Chokshi, Cannon, and Yoshida 2001). If observers help students, it's difficult to draw inferences about how well the lesson worked. It's important to let students know in advance that the extra teachers in the room will be studying the lesson, not helping the students. That way, students won't think they've encountered a roomful of exceptionally unhelpful adults!

Sharing Responsibilities

Given the many logistics involved in conducting a research lesson, you may want to divvy them up among group members, designating various tasks to different members:

- Obtain needed materials for the lesson.
- Copy the teaching-learning plan for observers.
- Take notes at the postlesson discussion.
- Facilitate the postlesson discussion.
- Keep the rest of the school informed.

	OBSERVING THE RESEARCH LESSON
1.	**Respect the classroom atmosphere.** For example, silence phones, refrain from side conversations, and arrive on time and stay for the entire lesson.
2.	**Do not help students or otherwise interfere with the natural flow of the lesson;** for example, be careful not to block students' view when they need to see the board or the teacher.
3.	**Collect data requested by the lesson planning team,** or focus on the "points to notice" laid out in their instructional plan. Prepare by reading the lesson plan thoroughly.
4.	**Focusing on the same student** (or pair of students) over the entire lesson is likely to yield the best picture of whether and how the students developed understanding.
5.	If the lesson study team concurs, it is all right to ask clarifying questions of a student **after the lesson is concluded.**

Figure 5-1 Guidelines for Observation of the Research Lesson

Because the teacher actually teaching the lesson already shoulders considerable responsibility, other group members may want to take responsibility for the support tasks. If your research lesson is to be observed by people beyond your immediate planning group, ask someone outside your planning group to facilitate the postlesson discussion.

Preparing for the Postlesson Discussion

Immediately following the lesson, it is important to give observers and planning members ten minutes or so before the debriefing to quietly reflect on the lesson and think about what they experienced and what they intend to share in the debriefing. Often teachers so enjoy the opportunity to closely observe students without responsibility for teaching that they want to share every detail of what they observed. This can result in a retell of the lesson from six different angles. Time to reflect before the postlesson discussion can help teachers focus and target their observations. A shared set of questions may also be helpful, for example:

- How did students' manipulative use relate to their problem solutions?
- Did the inferences made from primary source documents change over the course of the lesson?
- What questions about the text did students formulate during partner discussions?

Often these shared questions are developed in advance by the lesson study team, but sometimes interesting new questions emerge at the time of the research lesson. The lesson observation log provided in Appendix Q is organized with a broad column to record observations during the lesson and a narrow column to highlight particularly important observations. To avoid a long "laundry list" account, observers will want to select for discussion observations that are in some way revealing with respect to lesson goals or student learning. Packages of different-colored sticky notes may come in handy to flag and categorize key observations in your notes or in student work, so that you can easily find and share them.

Conducting the Postlesson Discussion

In Japan, there is a shared understanding of the nature and purpose of the discussion following a research lesson. U.S. teachers will need to create this shared understanding. Some strategies that might be helpful are:

- Post and review the agenda and ground rules for the discussion (see Figure 5–2), so that all attendees understand what kind of discussion is hoped for.
- Have a discussion chairperson who keeps time and facilitates, and agree in advance on how the facilitator will handle lengthy or inappropriate comments.
- Have a well-conceived plan for collecting and presenting data, so that a rich discussion is supported.

DISCUSSION OF THE RESEARCH LESSON	
1.	**The Instructor's Reflections**
	The instructor describes the aims for today's lesson, comments on how the lesson unfolded, including any surprises or difficulties, and reflects on what was learned in planning and conducting today's lesson (five minutes or less).
2.	**Background Information from the Lesson Study Group Members**
	The lesson study team members explain their goals for students (both lesson goals and long-term goals) and why they designed the lesson (and unit) as they did. They describe what they learned and any changes made to the lesson design over time.
3.	**Presentation and Discussion of Data from the Research Lesson**
	Lesson study team members (followed by observers, if any) present data from their observations, in order to answer questions developed by the team. The data may include student work, a verbatim record of questions by the teacher and/or students, narrative records of all activities by particular children or small groups, record of the blackboard, and so on. What do the data tell us about student thinking and learning, about lesson design, or about our goals? Data presentation is organized around the team's questions (including any new questions that arise during the research lesson) rather than as "laundry lists" or narratives.
4.	**General Discussion**
	A brief free discussion period, facilitated by a moderator, may be provided. The focus is on student learning and development and on how specific elements of lesson design promoted these (or not). The moderator may designate particular themes for discussion, so that there is ordered discussion of key issues, rather than a free-for-all. Comments of a sensitive nature may be conveyed privately at a later time.
5.	**Outside Commentator (optional)**
	An invited outside commentator may discuss the lesson's relation to key subject matter issues. Encourage the commentator to read "A Closer Look" on page 34.
6.	**Thanks**
	Be sure to thank the instructor, planners, and attendees for their work to improve instruction.

Figure 5–2 Guidelines for Discussion of the Research Lesson

- Have one group member take notes, which will later be used by the lesson study group to think about where to go next; "We've got that in our notes" can be a great way to move the discussion on. These notes will also be helpful in writing up the conclusion to the lesson plan.

- Say *our* rather than *my* or *your* when talking about the lesson. Reflect in speech that the research lesson belongs to the group, not just the teacher who taught it. The instructing teacher needs to feel supported!

In Japan, there are whole books devoted to the etiquette of lesson study discussion. No wonder! A U.S. teacher described feeling "naked" as she taught a research lesson in front of colleagues. A good agenda for the discussion can go a long way toward easing this sense of vulnerability and making the discussion safe and productive. Discussions of research lessons vary greatly in Japan, depending on the size and familiarity of the group attending the lesson, and whether it includes educators beyond those who planned the lesson. Figure 5–2 provides a sample protocol for the discussion that follows a research lesson. Several features are noteworthy:

- The teacher who actually taught the research lesson speaks first (briefly) and has the chance to point out any difficulties in the lesson before they can be pointed out by others. (And there seems to be an unwritten rule that teachers don't further criticize something that's already been identified as a problem.)

- The lesson belongs to the whole lesson study group. It is *our* lesson, not *my* lesson, and this is reflected in everyone's speech. Group members assume responsibility for explaining the thinking and planning behind the lesson.

- If observers from outside the lesson study group are present, the instructor or team members should talk about the lesson rationale, the differences between what they planned and what actually happened, and the aspects they want observers to discuss. It's always valuable to have observers from outside the lesson study group, as someone not involved in planning the lesson can look at it with fresh eyes.

- Discussion focuses on the data that participants were asked to collect during the lesson. Observers provide specific examples from the student work and conversations they recorded; they do not speak impressionistically about the quality of the lesson.

- It's not a ping-pong match; team members don't need to respond to every comment.

- Free discussion time is limited; hence there is limited opportunity for "grandstanding" and digression.

Although it may seem unwise to limit free discussion, Japanese teachers often note that the end of the formal discussion is "the beginning, not the end." They assume that discussions and individual feedback on the lesson will continue informally. As one teacher said (Lewis and Tsuchida 1998, p. 16) *after* the end of a research lesson discussion:

> The research lesson is not over yet. It's not a one-time lesson; rather, it gives me a chance to continue consulting with other teachers. For example, I may say to other teachers, "I want to ask you about my last lesson you saw...." We teachers can better connect with each other in this way.

At the end of a lesson study cycle, a teacher from Oakland, California, reflected:

> Colleagues see so much that I miss or that I don't focus on. This cycle has brought me closer to a few colleagues whom I normally don't associate with too much, and I'm a better teacher for it. I guess I ought to collaborate more broadly and more often.

This quote reminds us of lesson study's long-term goal: to create a group of colleagues who are able and motivated to work together to share and improve instruction.

Avoid the Twin Shoals of Happy Talk and Harping

Most of us have people in our lives—for example, a spouse, relative, or close friend—whom we value precisely because we know that person will give us honest feedback, in a supportive manner, when we ask for it. With careful work, a lesson study group can become this kind of ally. The group must navigate between two dangerous extremes: happy talk (where members say what they think others want to hear) and harping (where members show their smarts by deflating others). Educator Deborah Ball notes the value of disagreement:

> Masking disagreements hides individual struggles to practice wisely and so removes a good opportunity for learning. Politely refraining from critique and challenge, teachers have no forum for debating and improving their understandings. (Ball 1996, p. 505)

Asked what it is like to have research lessons criticized by colleagues, Japanese teachers often reply that critical feedback is a mark of respect. As one said, "Colleagues offer criticism because they expect you can improve, and because there is something in your teaching worth improving on. What would really be scary is if they remained silent."

When asked to sum up what had been learned from a cycle of lesson study, a U.S. educator wrote the following comments, which remind us of the importance of providing a postlesson discussion where different ideas can bump up against each other.

> I was struck today at the debrief by how much I disagreed with things that others said about the lesson or what they value/would have done differently and I really appreciate this opportunity to share differing points of view—even if in the end I disagree. I've learned a lot.

Reflect and Plan the Next Steps

You've now completed one cycle of lesson study, from thinking about your goals to bringing them to life in an actual lesson and reflecting on what went well and what needs further work. Now is the time to consider what your group would like to do next. Would you like to make further improvements in this lesson and try it in another classroom? Some groups revise and reteach each lesson more than once. (See "A Closer Look," page 63.) In planning a follow-up research lesson, it is often helpful to start with a review of student work from the previous lesson. It may help to sort student work into groups according to strategies or levels of understanding, and then examine the work further for patterns that give clues to how student thinking and learning develop. Some groups are amazed at the dramatic differences between the first and second teachings of a research lesson, produced by seemingly small modifications such as asking student groups to spread out across the room (where they were less likely to notice other groups' work and more likely to come up with novel solutions).

Did the lesson study cycle uncover issues you would like to address in a new lesson study cycle? This may be a good time to revisit the goals of your lesson study effort and your group's operating procedures. The following questions may help you reflect on the lesson study cycle and think about your next steps.[1]

---

1. These reflection questions are influenced by the work of Clea Fernandez and Makoto Yoshida with the Lesson Study Research Group.

A Closer Look: Why Reteach Lessons?

by Makoto Yoshida

Reteaching lessons gives teachers within a school more opportunities to teach in front of others and to observe lessons, other classrooms, and other students. Reteaching a lesson also enables teachers to see the impact of their discussion and revision of the lesson. After teaching a research lesson once, teachers can discuss the lesson in a more concrete fashion and on a deeper level and can approach its revision in a more thoughtful and systematic manner, based on actual observation of the students' learning process. Lesson observation and discussion with experienced teachers is particularly important for novice teachers, who have not yet developed good "eyes" and skills to observe lessons, and hence cannot think about how to reshape lessons to maximize student understanding.

Teachers from the Greenwich Japanese School in Connecticut and the Paterson Public School No. 2 in New Jersey voluntarily established a Math Lesson Study Circle in July 2001 and have been meeting at least once a month to jointly develop some lessons through lesson study. During these meetings, when the group is having difficulty resolving some issue in lesson design, the Japanese teachers have sometimes suggested teaching the lesson as it currently is and using the information from teaching the lesson to revise it. They have also mentioned that reteaching in a second classroom by a second teacher creates a totally different environment. Because there are no perfect lessons that are successful for every classroom situation, learning how to adjust a lesson is a valuable skill for teachers.

According to Japanese educators, reteaching increases opportunities for teachers to learn from one another, reveals the power for students of the revised lesson, and teaches valuable skills of lesson observation, discussion, and adaptation that are fundamental to improvement of teaching.

● ●

1. What did we learn about the subject matter and about the curriculum?

2. What did we learn about student thinking and about teaching?

3. Are we working together in a way that supports our learning and motivation? Do all members of our group feel included and valued? Do nonparticipants in our work feel informed and invited?

4. What insights did we gain from this lesson study cycle about productive habits in our learning practices as teachers, such as:

   • anticipation of student thinking

   • study and comparison of curriculum

   • drawing on outside knowledge resources (research, subject matter specialists, etc.)

   • careful observation of student learning

5. Is our work efficient? What is working well about our lesson study process and what needs to be changed?

If your meetings are not as productive as you wish, you might want to revisit earlier sections of this chapter and to consider ways to enhance the efficacy and efficiency of your work, such as:

1. Consult a content expert.

2. Review norms, and choose one to monitor and reflect on at each meeting.

3. At the end of each meeting, set tasks to accomplish at the next meeting.

4. Record minutes of your meeting and distribute them to group members before the next meeting.

5. Rotate roles such as facilitator, recorder, and timekeeper.

6. Use a preset meeting agenda (see Appendixes H and I) and clarify meeting goals at the outset of each meeting.

Take the Time to Share What You Have Learned

Lesson study developed into a schoolwide practice at Highlands School because the principal created opportunities for the early lesson study pioneers to share their work with colleagues—to make presentations at faculty meetings and to have colleagues observe and discuss research lessons. Lesson study has spread across the United States as teachers have presented their work in public lessons, at conferences, and in educational journals. Your teaching-learning plan and reflections on what the cycle has taught you about teaching and learning may constitute the core of a presentation, report, or journal article. You can find examples of such articles in *Language Arts*, where Jackie and fellow lesson study team member Lori Ricciardo-Musso shared their learning from a lesson study cycle on comprehension of expository text (Hurd and Ricciardo-Musso 2005) and in *History Teacher*, where Alameda County (California) teachers describe a lesson study cycle focused on student understanding of the economic and moral dimensions of slavery (Ogden, Perkins, and Donahue 2008). A PowerPoint template to organize presentation of your own lesson study work is included in the DVD accompanying this handbook.

Celebrate Your Learning

It takes courage for U.S. teachers to pioneer lesson study. Your lesson study group has taken risks to break down the walls that often isolate American teachers. Formal thanks from colleagues and administrators are in order. You have demonstrated your commitment to self-improvement in ways that may ripple through your school and beyond. Whatever else you do, be sure to congratulate and celebrate! Many U.S. groups have happily adopted the Japanese tradition of treating the lesson instructor to a happy hour or dinner out.

What Should You Expect from Lesson Study?

Lesson study keeps me on my toes, keeps me from getting complacent, keeps me challenged professionally. I compare it to the feeling I get when I am taking a graduate course. Lesson study allows me to build relationships with my colleagues. Lesson study opens the classroom doors and minimizes isolation.

—NICK TIMPONE, TEACHER, NEW YORK CITY

Figure 6–1 is designed to guide reflection after lesson study, and it summarizes the opportunities that well-designed lesson study should provide. This chapter briefly discusses each of the eight experiences in Figure 6–1.

> **Has lesson study provided an opportunity to:**
> - examine, build, and share our knowledge about teaching?
> - deepen our knowledge of subject matter?
> - develop our knowledge of students and student thinking?
> - see our own teaching through the eyes of students and colleagues?
> - think carefully about our goals in teaching a particular lesson, unit, and subject area?
> - ask and seek answers to our own pressing questions?
> - carefully consider our long-term goals for students?
> - build professional community?

Figure 6-1 Opportunities Provided by Well-Designed Lesson Study

Examine, Build, and Share Knowledge About Teaching

Daily, teachers must make many quick, subjective, solo judgments about what is working for their students. Lesson study creates a time and space for close, careful observation of student thinking and learning. Although lesson study sheds light on the effectiveness of particular lessons, it also builds and spreads knowledge of teaching strategies that can be applied throughout the curriculum, such as how to pose a challenging question or problem, how to support a good discussion, and how to foster student note taking and reflection. In "A Closer Look," Makoto Yoshida writes about the art of blackboard writing that has spread through lesson study in Japan.

As teachers watch and analyze research lessons, they develop a shared vocabulary for talking about the fine points of teaching and learning. Japanese teachers can name many techniques they have picked up through participation in research lessons, such as putting student names on magnets (so students can register on the board their agreement or disagreement with ideas under discussion, thereby allowing every student to see their thinking represented) and having students use hand signals to show whether they want to agree, disagree, or make a new point, allowing the discussion leader to manage the flow of discussion.

Examining Assumptions

Lesson study also provides an opportunity to examine familiar strategies more deeply. For example, even if we feel comfortable using cooperative groups in the classroom and think they are effective, lesson study allows us to examine a host of issues related to whether and in what circumstances this is actually so—for example, the benefits to various types of learners, how groups should be structured, and what needs to be in place for groups to work well. One lesson study group,

A Closer Look: Blackboard Use and Student Note Taking

by Makoto Yoshida

In U.S. mathematics lessons, there seems to be little emphasis on planning of blackboard use. Blackboards in U.S. classrooms are often covered with materials that are unrelated to the lesson, leaving very little space to write information vital to understanding the lesson. Multiple blackboards in different locations may be used, with the effect of scattering information, making it difficult for the students to know where to focus and distracting from the lesson's coherence. Information may be written and erased casually. In the United States, it seems blackboards are often used to demonstrate procedures but rarely to develop a mathematical idea using collective student ideas. When an overhead projector is used, much of the important information that will help students to learn the material disappears as soon as the switch is turned off.

In the case of Japanese mathematics lessons, the blackboard is used not just for posing problems, presenting student work, demonstrating solutions and procedures, and recording important mathematical concepts and formulas, but also for skillfully organizing students' thoughts and thought processes, recording ideas emerging from student discussion, and providing a summary of the lesson. In the minds of Japanese teachers, the blackboard is not simply a place to casually jot down important messages that they want the students to remember, but a tool to help organize student thinking and discussion to enhance the learning experience. Use of the blackboard is often planned during lesson study and becomes a topic for observation and discussion during the postlesson discussion.

What criteria do Japanese teachers use to plan and evaluate the use of the blackboard?

- From the board, is it easy for students and teacher to follow the flow of the lesson? Is the blackboard logically and coherently organized to help students understand the lesson?

- Are the goal and task of the lesson clear on the board?

- Does the board reflect students' voices, ways of thinking, and ideas?

- Does the board show how student ideas were challenged and developed through the class discussion?

- Are the materials presented on the board meaningful to students and effective for building their understanding of the lesson?

Japanese teachers sometimes comment that student note-taking skills reflect teachers' blackboard use. Students can't be expected to take good notes in their notebooks if they are not shown a model on the board. Many teachers prepare handouts at the beginning of the school year so the students can get used to taking notes. In the first trimester, the handout may include the story problem and spaces to write solutions, explanations, answers, and reflections on the lesson (for example, what they discovered, understood, and felt). Some teachers also ask students to write their friends' solutions and what they thought about those solutions as part of their explanations. As the year goes on, teachers gradually provide less guidance on the handouts and ask the students to produce similar notes in their own notebooks. Teachers often collect notebooks so they can be evaluated and suggestions can be made for improvement.

• •

exploring effective strategies for improving student comprehension during silent reading, decided to partner fluent readers with "less-ready" readers. During the postlesson discussion, one teacher commented that one of the less-ready students was "completely checked out" during the activity and "not even trying." Initially the classroom teacher explained this away by saying, "He's always like that—he never tries." Members of the lesson study team made conjectures about whether mixed-achievement pairs helped or hindered this student. The classroom teacher repeated the activity on a subsequent day, pairing students of similar reading skill. She discovered that the checked-out student was on task, engaged, and able to take the lead when paired with a student of similar reading skill. Cooperative groups and pairing became something to be analyzed carefully, rather than taken for granted, in the daily practice of these teachers.

Deepen Our Knowledge of Subject Matter

Mastery of content knowledge is essential to good teaching. Yet it is not obvious that traditional university course work helps teachers learn content in ways that readily transfer to teaching. A friend of ours humorously recalls what it felt like to learn science during the first year of medical school:

> Every week a renowned basic researcher would lecture us. It felt like each researcher filled up a huge dump truck with all the information that a future doctor might possibly need, backed it up to the lecture hall, and dumped it on the medical students. Minutes into each lecture, I fell asleep. Later I learned what I needed to know, not by crawling around to sift through all the dumped information, but by strategically figuring out what I needed to know to solve particular patients' cases and to understand particular diseases.
>
> (ANDREW LEAVITT, PERSONAL COMMUNICATION, 1978)

Leavitt's account highlights a problem common to doctors and teachers as clinicians: the danger of being overwhelmed by research and theory of unknown clinical relevance. Lesson study can help teachers in the way that treating patients helped the medical student, by providing a practical setting for identifying and trying out the information needed to solve a problem. As Liping Ma (2001) observed, "American educators assume that you need to know content knowledge *before* you can plan lessons. Chinese teachers think you learn content knowledge by planning lessons." Lesson study is full of opportunities for teachers to deepen their subject matter knowledge: as teachers jointly solve the task to be given students and compare their solutions; as they read and discuss standards, research articles, and the teachers' manual to write up their teaching-learning plan; as they consult content specialists during lesson planning or hear their comments on the research lesson. For example, members of the "How Many Seats?" lesson study team refined and strengthened their knowledge of the mathematical patterns in the problem, discovered the geometric reason for the plus-two pattern, and distinguished the meaning of several mathematical terms they had been using interchangeably (*rule, formula, equation*). Asked to reflect on the impact of her lesson study experience, one teacher said, "I have received huge gains in content knowledge. Often I go into a concept thinking I understand, and afterward I realize I only understood it superficially. Lesson study has taught me more sophisticated and varied ways to analyze work and to use student work to guide my teaching." Oakland, California, teacher Sue Scott (December 2010) summed up her experience with lesson study in history: "For me lesson study is you learn something at a deeper level and as a result of learning something at a deeper level, you can share that with your students."

Develop Our Knowledge of Students and Student Thinking

Lesson study gives teachers the chance to carefully observe a student over the course of an entire lesson and to understand student thinking. Teachers who understand students' thinking are better able to foster students' learning (Franke et al. 1998). For example, the teachers in the "How Many Seats?" lesson study cycle discovered that many students noticed the recursive pattern in the table (that adding one table adds one seat) but did not notice the functional pattern (there are always more two more seats than tables). They also noticed that some students revealed their thinking in their counting methods, and teachers used this information to redesign the lesson. High school history teachers conducting lesson study in Hayward, California, investigated how students drew on assigned primary and secondary sources on slavery when making arguments to peers. Teachers were able to identify the specific experiences that helped students move beyond a simplistic "good Northerners–bad Southerners" understanding of slavery to recognize slavery as an economic institution that benefited many Northerners as well as Southerners (Ogden, Perkins, and Donahue 2008).

Data collection during the research lesson enables teachers to see instruction through the eyes of the students: to trace what students understand or struggle with and to see what features of the lesson, classroom, and students themselves provide support or barriers to learning. Developing "the eyes to see children" is, in the view of many Japanese educators, the most important goal of lesson study. During research lessons, teachers scour the classroom for evidence about student learning, motivation, and behavior—everything from how students' thinking changed over the lesson to whether the quietist children spoke up to whether the students eagerly drew on their prior knowledge to solve a novel problem. Teachers improve their observational skills as they engage in lesson study. For example, a teacher may realize that he tends to miss students' nonverbal communication, compared with what fellow teachers notice. As teachers observe students' learning, behavior, and engagement during a research lesson, they can think more deeply about students than is usually possible in the hubbub of daily classroom life. In a class discussion, a first-year Mills College U.S. teacher commented (January 16, 2001) that lesson study "takes reflection to the next level; it makes it practical and tangible."

See Our Own Teaching Through the Eyes of Students and Colleagues

Improvement of teaching may require more than just acquiring new techniques and knowledge. Often it requires that we reexamine and revise our beliefs about learning and teaching. As teachers work together to plan or discuss a research lesson, their individual beliefs about teaching and learning become visible. Teachers' ideas bump up against each other, sparking reexamination of beliefs that otherwise might remain private. The teachers in the lesson study cycle "Improving Writing Through Lesson Study" video revealed their beliefs about a teacher's role in closing the achievement gap and grappled with the idea that all students can achieve to grade-level standards. (Discussion is available to view at www.youtube.com/watch?v=Ivfjp4Nrwg0 and www1.teachertube.com/members/viewVideo.php?video_id=217289&title=SMFC.) As we have participated in lesson study, we have seen shifts in our own and colleagues' beliefs about teaching and learning. One common shift is the recognition that students can benefit from grappling with challenging mathematics problems on which they are not immediately "successful."

Likewise, observation of students during a research lesson allows us to see our teaching through the eyes of our students. Teachers who planned a large public lesson in the Midwest were stunned when not a single student in the class used the procedure for calculating speed that the teacher had very carefully taught, and had students write down and practice, at the beginning of class. Instead, students used their own informal methods to solve the problem, completely ignoring the procedure that had been elegantly taught at the beginning of the lesson. To the teachers in the lesson study group and in the audience, it was a powerful demonstration that "you can't just give a child a tool; they need to ask for it, or at least see its connection to how they see the problem."

Similarly, by removing the worksheet and asking students do the hard intellectual work of organizing data, teachers in the video "How Many Seats?" learned that "it's important to have students do the work of the lesson, not the teachers." The *idea* that students need to do the thinking was probably not a new idea to the teachers in the group—indeed, it's almost a mantra these days. But seeing the difference between the two lessons jolted these teachers to examine the tacit beliefs underlying their design of the first lesson and underlying their daily instruction. Without shared classroom experiences and principled discussion of what is observed, it may be easy for teachers' beliefs about good instruction to remain encapsulated, safely out of reach of influence from practice and colleagues.

Think Carefully About the Goals of a Particular Lesson, Unit, and Subject Area

Lesson study gives teachers the chance to think carefully about what they want students to learn from a particular lesson, unit, and subject area. As one teacher said (Lewis 2002, p. 28):

> Research lessons are very meaningful for teachers because . . . we think hard and in a fundamental way about several critical issues. For example: What is the basic goal of this lesson in this textbook? How does this particular lesson relate to my students' learning and progress in this school year? How does this lesson relate to other curriculum areas? Thus, it is very beneficial to teachers. Unless we think about all these things, we can't conduct research lessons. That is the purpose or significance of research lessons. Even if teachers do not think hard about the lessons they teach daily from the textbook, they must really re-think the fundamental issues for research lessons.

As Chapter Six explores in detail, lesson study is *not just about a single lesson*. The research lesson provides a window on the teaching of an entire unit and subject area, and indeed, on student development more broadly. As New York educator, Nick Timpone, described the impact of lesson study on his instruction:

> The most notable change in my lesson planning and teaching has been the questions that I ask myself. The first question I ask myself about a lesson is "What do I want the students to learn from this lesson?" Although this may seem an obvious question to ask, it was never something I asked myself until I began the lesson study process. The question I was asking myself before lesson study was more like "What am I covering today?"

Ask and Seek Answers to Our Own Pressing Questions

Lesson study does something that is a little bit scary and yet liberating for teachers. It acknowledges that the answers we seek aren't "out there" in the form of a perfect program or expert who can tell us exactly how to do things. Excellent programs, experts, and research are important starting places, but the answers we seek can be found only by looking closely at what our students are saying, doing, and thinking in our classrooms. Lesson study begins with our questions, rather than someone else's answers. As "A Closer Look" reveals, lesson study not only allows us to investigate questions of interest to us, it provokes new questions. What began as a straightforward look at the teaching of a lesson from a popular, nationally recognized spelling program ended by provoking big questions about what students were actually learning.

A Closer Look: The Power of Group Observation

When the faculty at Highlands School elected to study differentiation of instruction, one lesson study group started by observing a spelling lesson that was taught each year at the school and that, in the view of group members, already incorporated successful differentiation strategies. One team member volunteered to teach the lesson while the other four team members individually collected data on particular groups of students during the lesson: second-language learners and students achieving at a low, average, or high level. Prior to the lesson, the teachers shared their individual impressions of how the lesson met the needs of varied students. One teacher had found the lesson stimulating and engaging for her high-performing students, another commented that it provided important scaffolding for her second-language students, and a third remarked that the lesson provided access for all students to gain knowledge. The teachers unanimously agreed that the students found the lesson "fun" and "engaging."

Following the research lesson, the team shared the data they had collected during the lesson. The high-achieving students were off-task for 50 percent of the lesson while waiting for other students to catch up; the second-language students and lower-achieving students had the wrong answer more than half of the time; and the average-achieving students showed no noticeable gain in skills by the end of the lesson. A postlesson survey confirmed that students thought the activity was fun, but that they could not articulate what they had learned. The teachers were stunned. Their on-the-fly observations of students in their own classes had lulled them into thinking the lesson was successful because students seemed to be engaged and enjoying it. The fact that they were using a popular and nationally recognized spelling program had no doubt contributed to the feeling that the activity must be beneficial. Data collected during the research lesson, however, led the teachers to reevaluate the activity and to realize that a nationally known program plus fun and engagement do not necessarily add up to student learning.

Lesson study not only allows us to investigate questions of interest to us, it provokes new questions. What began as a straightforward look at the teaching of a lesson from a popular spelling program ended by provoking big questions about what students were actually learning.

Carefully Consider Our Long-Term Goals for Students

Lesson study starts when teachers agree upon a shared goal for improvement—a "research theme" or "important aim." To many U.S. educators, the opportunity to consider long-term goals feels like the essential missing piece of instructional improvement. As one student teacher from Mills College, Oakland, California, commented: "Lesson study focuses on the long term; usually when you're teaching you don't have time to think beyond the immediate skills you want students to learn that day" (January 12, 2001). Another Mills College student teacher noted: "A lot of [American] schools develop mission statements, but we don't do anything with them. The mission statements get put in a drawer and then teachers become cynical because the mission statements don't go anywhere. Lesson study gives guts to a mission statement, makes it real, and brings it to life" (January 12, 2001).

Building lesson study around long-term goals may offer protection against faddism and trivial goals. The long-term focus enables teachers to keep firmly in mind the qualities such as curiosity and persistence that are likely to be essential to students' long-term academic development. The research theme reminds us that, over the long term, learning is greatly shaped by students' interest, motivation, sense of support from classmates, and other qualities of heart and mind. For example, in the levers lesson shown on the video "Can You Lift 100 Kilograms?" (www.lessonresearch.net), Japanese teachers gathered data on students' *tsubuyaki* (under-breath exclamations) and indicators of interest such as students' "shining eyes." Teachers reasoned that surprise and amazement about the lever's power would motivate students to understand its principles.

The question that animates whole-school lesson study—"What qualities do we hope our students have when they leave our school?"—is a question that is likely to be deeply motivating to every teacher. It provides a way to connect daily lessons to our most cherished long-term goals for students. To the extent that lesson study's long-term goals connect us to that larger educational purpose, they will provide motivational fuel. A Mills College student teacher noted: "I really like how lesson study is connected to a larger goal; even the tiny details of the lesson don't seem mundane, because they are connected to a larger goal" (January 23, 2001).

Perhaps you are interested in lesson study primarily as a way to improve instruction *now*, not in students' qualities five years from now. Even so, you will find it worthwhile to think about the qualities you would like your students to have five years in the future. You'll probably find that mathematics, language arts, and every other subject are inseparable from your broader goals for students. U.S. researchers were surprised to find that Japanese teachers began *mathematics* lesson study with the question "What kind of children do we want to raise in this school?" (Fernandez, Chokshi, Cannon, and Yoshida 2001). But it should not be so surprising. Qualities like curiosity, persistence, organization, and responsibility heavily influence student learning of mathematics, language arts, and other subjects. At the same time, daily lessons heavily influence development of these important qualities.

The gold standard for judging the research lesson is how students are responding and learning—not whether teachers are using the fashionable teaching strategy of the moment. James Stigler and James Hiebert write:

Reform documents that focus teachers' attention on features of "good teaching" in the absence of supporting contexts might actually divert attention away from

the more important goals of student learning. They may inadvertently cause teachers to substitute the means for the ends—to define success in terms of specific features or activities instead of long-term improvements in learning.

(STIGLER AND HIEBERT 1999, 107–108)

Theory and research provide excellent starting points for understanding what good instruction is, and, in a perfectly controlled world, the "best practices" documented by research might be the same in every classroom. But in the real world, every class is different. Lesson study assumes that teachers need to look for evidence of students' learning, motivation, and development in their own classrooms and does not assume that a strategy will work automatically simply because it has been "proven" through research.

Build Professional Community

"Isolation is the enemy of improvement" notes educator Richard Elmore (1999–2000). Although the average Japanese teacher sees and discusses about ten research lessons a year (Yoshida 1999), U.S. teachers typically have few opportunities to observe and discuss lessons taught by others. A veteran U.S. elementary teacher routinely advises her student teachers: "Observe as many teachers as you possibly can during your student teaching year. This is the last time in your career you will have the chance!" Even if U.S. teachers invest time in collaboration, not every collaborative experience yields dividends in the classroom. Because lesson study focuses on shared practical work to improve lessons, it has the potential to benefit students directly while at the same time building collaboration among teachers.

Lesson study demands a different quality and intensity of collaboration than do most other professional activities. For example, working with grade-level colleagues to hammer out a shared yearlong curriculum plan may require a bit of negotiation, but it does not involve the steady give-and-take and challenge to one's beliefs about teaching, learning, and subject matter that teachers routinely encounter in lesson study. Lesson study collaboration isn't just about working with other teachers so that you aren't isolated anymore; it's about collaboration that influences you as an educator. It takes you out of your classroom and forces you to look inside yourself. Lesson study transforms individual teachers and the community in which they work, allowing them to draw on one another's knowledge. As Jackie says, "Lesson study changes me; some other collaborative activities don't."

The collaboration that occurs in lesson study has ripples throughout the school culture, as teachers become willing to open their classrooms and admit their struggles. Lesson study breaks down isolation and rebuts the myth that teachers enter teaching with all the knowledge they need. When Highlands School shifted its lesson study focus to language arts after several years of work in mathematics, Jackie was struck by how much the school culture had changed through lesson study; teachers immediately admitted their challenges related to teaching writing. In a similar vein, Massachusetts high school teacher Joanne

Tankard Smith summed up lesson study, "Great trust has developed over time that allows us to be both teachers and learners with each other. Isn't that what it's all about?" (Gorman 2010).

Lesson study also provides a natural way for teachers to think about how their own teaching connects with what other teachers are doing. Teacher Heather Crawford reflects on lesson study's impact at Paterson School No. 2, in Paterson, New Jersey:

> In the past, a lot of us never really thought about two grades down the line and how what we were teaching affects them. And now we really are. We are looking at it from [the point of view of] "This is what they learn in kindergarten. How does it carry through eighth grade?"

Lesson study thus provides opportunities for articulation across the grades, offering teachers a clearer picture of how the curriculum they teach underlies what students learn in subsequent years, ensuring a more coherent experience for students. A fourth-grade teacher watching a fifth-grade geometry lesson was disturbed to find that students could not remember or use formulas for perimeter and area they had studied in her class the prior year. When students fail to use information they have "learned," it provides us with important feedback. When talking about the impact of lesson study at her school, Becky Pittard of Volusia County, Florida, told the following story about a lesson study group at her school that included kindergarten through grade 5 teachers:

> We were doing a lesson on the equal sign and traced how the idea "is the same as" develops from kindergarten matching activities all the way to equations with multiple operations and variables on both sides of the equal sign. As the kindergarten teacher, PJ Maccio, leaned back in her chair looking at how the concept evolved across the grade levels, she remarked, with quite a bit of sass in her voice, that if she hadn't laid the foundation for the meaning of "same as," then the rest of us would not have had an easy time teaching "equality." There was a confident grin on her face as she announced the importance of her work. While we all laughed with her, we acknowledged she was absolutely correct.

Lesson study reminds us that, over the long term, the quality of students' learning depends upon the quality of collaboration among a school-full of teachers—not just the excellence of a few.

Summary

Because lesson study represents a substantial departure from the professional learning approaches familiar to most of us, it is important to examine whether it provides the opportunities described in this chapter. Establishing these opportunities is the key to successful lesson study. As teachers articulate their long-term goals for students and investigate their own pressing questions about student learning, a shift will occur. Teachers will have a learning system that allows them to collaboratively make sense of new ideas from inside and outside the school—not just the big contours, but the nitty-gritty of classroom enactment and the subtle changes in student responses that augur change. Teachers will have a system that enables them to learn daily from colleagues and students as well as from research and from external experts. Chapter Seven explores the diverse, interlocking forms of lesson study that, together, can allow instructional improvement on a regional and national basis.

chapter 7

Lesson Study's Diverse Forms: Mobilizing Lesson Study for Regional and National Improvement

Good teaching is very easy to talk about, but very hard to do.

—AKIHIKO TAKAHASHI, ASSOCIATE PROFESSOR OF EDUCATION, DEPAUL UNIVERSITY

This chapter explores diverse forms of lesson study and argues that these different forms of lesson study can together produce a comprehensive system for instructional improvement across a region. As Figure 7–1 illustrates, Japan has just such a system of interlocking, synergistic lesson study activities. Nationally and regionally active educators teach large public research lessons attended by district and school subject matter specialists, who bring new approaches of interest back to their own region and try them out in lesson study there. District- and school-based groups study how the new ideas work in their local context, often honing and improving them in the process, and opening up their own work in public research lessons if they so choose. Independent

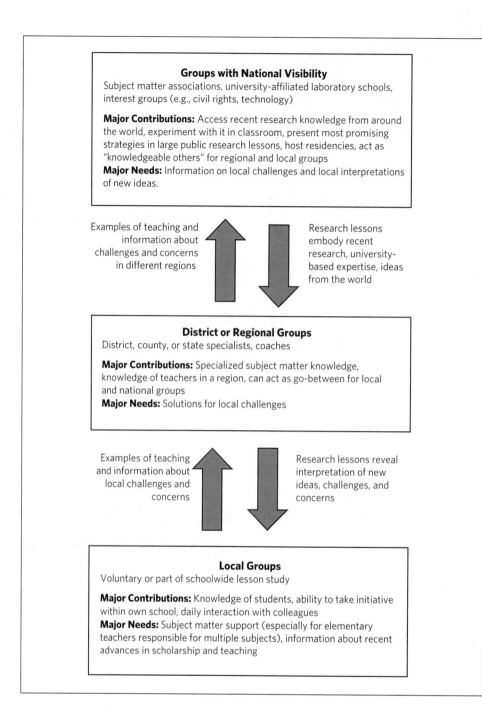

Groups with National Visibility
Subject matter associations, university-affiliated laboratory schools, interest groups (e.g., civil rights, technology)

Major Contributions: Access recent research knowledge from around the world, experiment with it in classroom, present most promising strategies in large public research lessons, host residencies, act as "knowledgeable others" for regional and local groups
Major Needs: Information on local challenges and local interpretations of new ideas.

Examples of teaching and information about challenges and concerns in different regions

Research lessons embody recent research, university-based expertise, ideas from the world

District or Regional Groups
District, county, or state specialists, coaches

Major Contributions: Specialized subject matter knowledge, knowledge of teachers in a region, can act as go-between for local and national groups
Major Needs: Solutions for local challenges

Examples of teaching and information about local challenges and concerns

Research lessons reveal interpretation of new ideas, challenges, and concerns

Local Groups
Voluntary or part of schoolwide lesson study

Major Contributions: Knowledge of students, ability to take initiative within own school, daily interaction with colleagues
Major Needs: Subject matter support (especially for elementary teachers responsible for multiple subjects), information about recent advances in scholarship and teaching

Figure 7-1 Different Types of Lesson Study Together Create a Comprehensive Improvement System

professional organizations focused on a wide range of topics—from whole language to problem-solving-centered instruction—provide a conduit for new ideas from around the world to be examined and tested by classroom teachers, often working in collaboration with university-based researchers.

Different types of lesson study are beginning to emerge in North America as well, allowing knowledge to spread across schools and districts. The example of regional spread of reengagement highlighted in Chapter One illustrates how ideas spread from a regional lesson study network of mathematics coaches to individual schools' lesson study groups. In this chapter, we take a closer look at the different types of lesson study in order to understand how they can work synergistically across a region or even a nation.

1. *A Small, Voluntary Lesson Study Group: A Good Place to Start.* Lesson study is a change in culture. So we often recommend that educators interested in building lesson study in their school or district start by trying it themselves, with a small group of interested colleagues. Chapter Two recounts how Jackie and colleagues started a small, voluntary lesson study effort that eventually supported the development of local, schoolwide, and regional lesson study. Once lesson study group members develop comfort and some degree of skill with the lesson study process, they provide a local example of lesson study culture for other local educators to "visit." Cultures are most easily understood by immersing oneself (not just by reading). So small, voluntary lesson study groups can establish a toehold for the new ideas lesson study entails. Lesson study pioneers can establish a base camp so that others can explore, and perhaps settle, in a new territory.

2. *Lesson Study in a Summer Institute.* The "How Many Seats?" lesson study cycle occurred in the context of a summer mathematics institute. A perennial challenge for institute organizers is how to help participants carry their learning from an institute into their daily teaching. Jackie and her colleagues often design lesson study into summer institutes, "borrowing" classes from year-round schools or summer schools for research lessons. An advantage of doing lesson study during a summer institute is freedom from other pressures of the teaching year and the opportunity to concentrate intensely on lesson study. A disadvantage is teaching students one does not know well, although teachers sometimes get around this by inviting back their prior year's students for a summertime lesson. Lesson study practiced during a summer institute can provide an opportunity for teachers to conduct in-depth investigation of a particular topic (for example, algebra in the elementary curriculum) or to study and test out recent advances in research or new curriculum materials.

3. *Lesson Study Embedded in School-Year Professional Development.* Stan Pesick and Shelly Weintraub, history–social studies coaches in Oakland, California, saw lesson study in action in mathematics and decided to include a lesson study component in their application for a Teaching American History grant from the U.S. government. Oakland's teachers of American history (grades 5, 8, and 11) can apply to the district's program of historical study and research for teachers. Teachers participate in presentations by nationally known historians and develop their own inquiry questions, working with history graduate students to research these questions. (See www.teachingamericanhistory.us.)

Lesson study is the bridge that enables these Oakland teachers to bring their own experiences of historical scholarship into their classroom instruction; in small groups, teachers collaboratively plan a classroom lesson, which one or more members of the team teach to their students. The research lesson is observed by team members, by district history–social studies specialists, and sometimes by historians as well. Teachers build many different kinds of bridges from their own professional learning experiences into their teaching. From their own research experience, some teachers become interested in how students use primary source documents and focus their inquiry on understanding and supporting students' use of photographs, diaries, and other primary source materials. Other teachers become interested in a particular issue discussed by a historian and decide to explore it with their students; for example, a presentation on historical changes in the concept of "freedom" led a group of teachers to ask how their students understand freedom in historical texts and in the present day. In each case, lesson study provides a time and structure to systematically draw out the lessons from one's own professional learning experiences and figure out, with colleagues, how they can inform classroom instruction.

4. *Schoolwide Lesson Study.* Chapter Two tells the story of lesson study's emergence at Highlands Elementary School, where it grew from a small group of teachers to the whole faculty. At Highlands School and other U.S. schools practicing lesson study on a schoolwide basis, typically the whole faculty chooses a schoolwide research theme that provides a common focus for the work, and then teachers break up into lesson study groups of three to six teachers who conduct two cycles of lesson study per year and share their learnings with the whole faculty at regular intervals. All the teachers in the school may read a book or article and use their lesson study work to develop in practice, share, and refine ideas or strategies suggested by the reading. In the overall ecology of lesson study, an important strength of schoolwide lesson study is the capacity to bring on board all teachers within a school, building coherence across classrooms and changing the culture of learning among adults.

One year, schoolwide lesson study at Highlands School focused on the new state mathematics standards, and each grade level chose one standard on which to focus its lesson study work. Kindergarten teachers at Highlands School chose a standard that they originally thought was too challenging for kindergarteners: "Students use concrete objects to determine the answer to addition and subtraction problems." However, as the teachers investigated this standard in their lesson study work, they realized that tasks that ask students to decompose numbers (for example, find different ways to make 5) brought this standard well within the grasp of their students (Murata 2010). Lesson study provided the vehicle for these teachers to broaden their image of "addition and subtraction problems" and to realize that the standard could be successfully enacted if approached through decomposition activities. As each grade-level team shared its work around a mathematics standard, teachers across the school began to see how their work supported and depended on the work of other teachers.

5. *Lesson Study by Groups of Coaches or Specialists.* When specialists—subject matter coaches, professional developers, researchers—get together to conduct lesson study, it sends a powerful message about the importance of continued learning, the significance of teaching, and the fact that answers to the problems of practice are not all known. When these specialists also participate in school-based lesson study groups (as lesson study team members or as outside commentators), they can share what they have learned from their own lesson study work, as well as educate themselves about the challenges faced by educators in various school settings. Joint participation by coaches and subject matter specialists in lesson study provides a much more level playing field between "providers" and

A Closer Look: Lessons from the History Classroom

by Matthew Karlsen, Educational Service District 112, Vancouver, Washington, and Peter Thacker, University of Portland

As leaders of a Teaching American History grant, we routinely share with teachers a set of strategies for using primary source documents:

- Select documents based on the insight they provide into specific content.
- Anticipate student challenges in understanding the documents and take steps to mitigate the challenges.
- Design lessons that support student reading and interpretation.
- Carefully examine the documents themselves before giving them to students.

What *we* say, however, is not nearly as important as what teachers themselves notice as they teach and observe the research lesson. For example, a group of middle school teachers taught a lesson designed to have eighth graders unveil arguments about The Stamp Act. Students read William Pitt's address to Parliament, as posted on a popular resource website. When asked to highlight from the document arguments for and against The Stamp Act, students were unable to do so meaningfully.

The postlesson discussion allowed teachers to freshly consider the strategies for using primary source documents presented in our workshops, in light of their own observations of students. Working within a trusted, thoughtful group of colleagues, teachers were able to acknowledge that the approach used in the lesson did not meet students' needs and to search for solutions. In future iterations, they would prep the document differently, rewrite the document introduction and title, pare down the reading, and support student comprehension by asking students to identify unknown words and phrases. Together, these changes supported students in grasping the attitudes about The Stamp Act lurking in the text.

As leaders of a professional learning program, this experience reminded us that the research lesson prompted learning that our words alone did not. Teaching and observing a research lesson with colleagues, and seeing students struggle, prompt self-reflection and retooling.

• •

"consumers" of professional development than is typical in many professional learning settings. "A Closer Look" reveals how leaders of professional development who incorporate lesson study are often struck by the powerful feedback it provides, revealing what messages teachers have actually taken away from workshops and presentations.

6. *Lesson Study as Mentoring for New Teachers.* Barbara Scott, a math coach and mentor for new teachers in the San Mateo-Foster City School District, arranged for the new teachers she mentored to become part of a lesson study group in which she participated. In this way, she was able to work intensively with these new teachers while at the same time supporting their connections to other colleagues and setting up the expectation that learning to improve instruction would be a long-term part of their teaching career, not just something for the first few years. The lesson study group also enabled the new teachers to share their knowledge from recent training with colleagues at their school sites, creating a two-way street in which they could contribute as well as receive knowledge.

One of the school sites Barbara Scott mentored was a "Program Improvement" school with very high teacher turnover. Lesson study not only helped network new and veteran teachers but also provided an avenue for teachers to reconcile the many mandated programs they were required to implement. Given the many stringent requirements on Program Improvement schools, teachers often complain of feeling powerless in a stream of scripted programs. Through the process of lesson study, these teachers found a way to focus on the needs of their students while thoughtfully utilizing these programs.

7. *Lesson Study in Preservice Education.* A number of preservice teacher education programs now include lesson study (e.g., Cossey and Tucher 2005; Murata and Pothen, forthcoming). In these programs, preservice students are able to work together to connect what is learned in their university classes with what happens in an actual classroom lesson; they learn early in their careers the skills and benefits of collaboration; and they learn the power of observation and analysis of student thinking and begin to develop the skills to conduct it. Links to programs that use lesson study in the education of aspiring teachers can be found at www.lessonresearch.net/preservice.html.

8. *Public Lessons as Part of a Regional or National Conference.* Large public lessons now occur regularly during annual conferences in several regions of the United States, including Northern California, Chicago, and New York. Often lessons are taught both by local teachers and also by teachers with a national or international reputation who have been invited for the occasion. Organizations such as the National Council of Teachers of Mathematics have also had public research lessons taught as sessions within an annual conference. In the San Francisco Bay Area, the Kabcenell Foundation and Silicon Valley Mathematics Initiative for a number of years have made grants available to lesson study teams in districts across the region. Each lesson study team receives a grant (about $3,000 for substitutes and release time) and partners up with another lesson study team in the program. After observing each other's research lessons during a fall lesson study cycle, the teams go on to share what they learned (often in the form of public research lessons) at a regional conference that brings together teams from twenty or more districts around the region. Research on the Silicon Valley Mathematics Initiative documents the spread of knowledge for teaching across school and district borders (Lewis et al. 2012).

Public lessons that occur during regular annual or biennial conferences—sponsored by professional organizations, subject matter specialists' organizations, university laboratory schools, and other groups—have been a major force in reshaping Japanese elementary education. District coaches and specialists visit these conferences and bring back ideas they like to their own local lesson study work. Research lessons conducted at regional and national conferences can spread ideas across a large region.

Contrasts Among Types of Lesson Study

The different types of lesson study afford different possibilities and constraints. In a small, voluntary group, teachers interested in pioneering lesson study can do so, working only with a highly motivated group of colleagues. But in a schoolwide effort, teachers see the impact of their work magnified, because their learning can be put to use throughout the school. Conversations change as teachers know what their colleagues mean by terms like *problem solving*, and human relationships change as teachers work together to bring to life a shared educational vision throughout a school. In a group that contains only math coaches, members can go further and faster in developing their content knowledge, but in a group that includes both a math coach and full-time classroom teachers, there is more opportunity for new ideas about mathematics instruction to spread to teachers who might not otherwise seek out these ideas.

The different reaches of lesson study—from local to national—create possibilities for diffusion of ideas across a region and a nation. We have seen ideas spread across many kinds of boundaries: between elementary and secondary schools; across districts; between foundation, university, and school personnel; and between Japanese and U.S. teachers (Lewis and Perry 2009/2010; Lewis et al. 2012). Chapter One described the regional spread of the reengagement strategy through lesson study. Teachers in various districts picked up the reengagement strategy and honed it for use with their pressing problems—for example, what to do when small-group discussions seemed to be cementing students' misunderstandings. In each case, lesson observers gathered data on students that revealed the impact of the reengagement strategy on student learning.

Together, the different types of lesson study outlined in this chapter enable educators to develop, refine, and spread knowledge for teaching. These varied types of lesson study together constitute a system for "scale up" of innovation that has many advantages over centrally planned and controlled rollout of an innovation. Teachers can collaborate to bring the innovation to life and help one another develop the knowledge needed to use it—knowledge that may not be anticipated by planners of a centralized innovation. Teachers can adapt and refine the innovation to varied local settings, using careful observation of students during research lessons to assess their adaptations. Research lessons provide a shared playing field for school-based educators, university-based educators, coaches, administrators, policy makers, foundation personnel, and others to see the innovation in action and discuss how it fits (or does not fit) their respective visions. Because teachers take an active role in seeking and testing innovations that meet their needs, innovations will be "pulled in" by teachers rather than "pushed in" by outsiders, leveraging the power of teachers and their networks.

Misconceptions, Challenges, and Frequently Asked Questions

All who practice lesson study should take responsibility for thinking about how to further improve our translation of this practice in the United States. We need more opportunities to learn from others around the country who are engaged in this very powerful professional learning practice.

—MARY PAT O'CONNELL, PRINCIPAL, NIXON ELEMENTARY SCHOOL, PALO ALTO, CALIFORNIA

This chapter begins with a group of questions asked so frequently that we have broken them out for quick discussion here, although earlier chapters of the book address these questions more fully. Following the frequently asked questions, we discuss common misconceptions about lesson study.

Frequently Asked Questions

1. Can videotape be substituted for live observation of research lessons?

Videotape offers certain advantages over live observation of research lessons, such as flexibility of scheduling and the possibility of repeated viewing. Some teachers feel more comfortable being videotaped (with the knowledge that they can later choose not to share the video) than being observed live. It's a great idea to videotape your group's research lesson, but as a supplement to live observation, not a substitute for it.

Live research lessons are the heart of lesson study in Japan, and teachers sometimes travel hundreds of miles to attend them. Why do Japanese teachers accord so much importance to live observation? When teachers watch a research lesson, they notice many things that cannot be gathered from student tests, written work, or even videotapes. For example, teachers may document an entire lesson from the perspective of a given student, noting when that student tuned in and out, how the student interacted with peers, and how the student interpreted the teacher's instructions. Students' engagement, persistence, interactions within small groups, and *tsubuyaki* (under-breath exclamations) may offer important insights into what worked and what did not during the lesson. Live observation allows teachers to record the participation of all students, scan the room for evidence that students understand a task, closely study the work of individual students and groups, and pick up variations in the mood and interest level in the classroom. Videographers must decide (often in advance of the lesson) where to focus the camera(s), and this inevitably narrows the stream of experience captured on tape. In contrast, live observation enables teachers to follow the "swiftly flowing river" of instruction in unanticipated directions.

Sherrilynn Rawson, principal of Nellie Muir Elementary, an Oregon school that practices lesson study schoolwide, recalls that it was a big change when she and her faculty went from looking at student work to observing research lessons. "We had been looking at student work, but didn't realize how important it was to look at students while they were *doing* the work." During a first-grade lesson study cycle focused on helping students learn how to edit their writing, teachers at Nellie Muir Elementary noticed the power of observing students as they actually edited their work. Teachers were able to see how students used a step-by-step approach to editing—what kinds of editing students did well and what they still needed to learn about the editing process. As teachers adopted in their own classrooms the practice of carefully observing students *doing* their work, they made some surprising discoveries: for example, sometimes drawing interfered with students solving particular mathematics problems, rather than offering support. This interesting discovery became the focus of a subsequent lesson study cycle in mathematics.

Videotape, audiotape, lesson plans, photographs, and student work are all excellent methods to document research lessons. If possible, use all of them to capture your lesson study work.

2. What can administrators do to support lesson study?

Lesson study is a teacher-led process. However, administrators' support can be crucial in many ways, including:

- locating resources such as time, money, and knowledge sources (both people and materials) to deepen the work

- helping to develop and protect a schedule for the work (see page 41)

- building a shared vision about how lesson study will help teachers address the issues of importance to individual teachers and the whole faculty (as discussed in the case of Highlands School in Chapter Two)

- protecting teachers from overload by using lesson study to focus on the most pressing issues facing teachers and the school

- affirming the importance of the lesson study work and expectation that its impact will grow gradually over time

- ensuring that lesson study groups present and share their work

In lesson study, teachers learn through collaborative investigation and research. For most educators, this is a paradigm shift from professional development in which teachers are told or shown by experts, and in which the teacher's role is mainly to listen, take notes, and practice classroom activities designed by others. Administrators may find it hard to acknowledge the professional capacity of teachers to be successful at collaborative investigation and research and may give up quickly when rough spots are encountered—for example, when a research lesson points up gaps in teachers' understanding of subject matter or a group sticks to a style of teaching that is comfortable and familiar. When administrators themselves take a learning stance, they can help create school cultures where such a stance is valued and where teachers expect to ask and be asked difficult questions and to persist in improving practice. A good place for administrators to begin the learning stance is to become acquainted with the lesson study process described in Chapters Three through Five, especially elements such as the protocol for postlesson discussion, which are likely to be a shift in culture.

Lesson study is most likely to flourish in an environment in which teachers choose to participate, in which they bring their own pressing questions and classroom challenges to the table, and in which they feel some agency (rather than feeling that they are marching through steps designed by someone else). A skillful administrator will help teachers connect their pressing questions and classroom challenges to high-quality knowledge resources and an overall vision of progress for the school, as Mary Pat O'Connell did at High-

A Closer Look: A Principal's Perspective

by Mary Pat O'Connell

I'd like to add my voice to that of the authors in encouraging teachers and administrators to learn about lesson study and give it a try. In the seven years that I worked with Jackie and Catherine to introduce and refine the practice of lesson study in our school, I witnessed the growth and development of a highly effective professional learning community. Although difficult to accurately attribute the cause of change, during this same time period, our students' performance improved on a variety of measures while the gap between the achievement levels of our subpopulations declined (Lewis et al. 2006).

We approached our work using lesson study with the parallel goals of researching the impact of specific instructional strategies on our students' learning and, at the same time, translating, evaluating, and refining the Japanese model of lesson study into a professional learning practice that is effective in the context of an American elementary school.

As principal, I learned a tremendous amount over the years about effective teaching practices from our shared research through lesson study. We investigated instructional strategies within a variety of broad categories including standards-based instruction, differentiation, support for socioeconomically disadvantaged students and English learners, and so on. I did not simply watch lesson study occur at my school, but actively participated in the planning, observing, and reflecting that occurred in the various teams. I participated in all of the behind-the-scenes planning for our professional learning sessions, including the crafting of our suggested agendas. If instructional leadership is to mean anything, a principal must be just as engaged in learning as the teachers.

Our practice of lesson study also evolved over this time period. We began with only the simplest understanding of the model and developed confidence in our ability to adjust and refine our practice to improve our own learning. The practice of lesson study within a school should grow naturally from the base of excited early adopters who encourage the participation of their peers. I doubt that it can be effective if simply imposed on a staff by the administrator. The quality of learning is directly related to the interest and commitment of the learners. The more the teachers research and seek input, the better foundation they have for their research lessons and the greater the depth of understanding their discussions will produce.

· ·

lands School (see Chapter Two). Lesson study groups connected their work to an overarching shared goal, such as closing the achievement gap by investigating and improving techniques for reaching struggling learners. The following quote suggests that the kind of leadership required for lesson study has been recognized for at least a few thousand years.

To lead people, walk beside them . . . As for the best leaders, the people do not notice their existence. The next best, the people honor and praise. The next, the people fear; and the next, the people hate. . . . When the best leader's work is done, the people say, "We did it ourselves!"

(LAO-TSU)

3. What is the best way to scale up lesson study?

As emphasized throughout, teachers play a central role in lesson study, so their thinking and initiative must be central to any scale-up plan. Mandated participation is problematic for a process that requires so much leadership and disclosure from teachers, so it is usually preferable to begin with some willing groups of pioneers and plan opportunities for them to share their work. Chapter Two describes how lesson study grew from one group to schoolwide at Highlands School. The best introduction to lesson study is to see it in action. There are now regular conferences and workshops where teachers can participate in research lessons conducted by experienced groups, or you can put out a listserv inquiry to find a group near you that can accommodate visitors at a research lesson (lsnetwork@mailman.depaul.edu). Starting with teachers who volunteer and giving them a year or more to build their own comfort and skill with lesson study may be more effective, in the long run, than trying to start with all educators at a site. The regional mathematics lesson study network in the San Francisco–Silicon Valley Region provides a powerful model for the spread of lesson study (and of improvements to mathematics instruction) across a region, through integration of lesson study within a regional coaching network with a strong set of opportunities for subject matter learning (Lewis et al. 2012; Foster and Poppers 2009).

4. What should be the focus of lesson study evaluation?

We recommend an approach that includes both formative (process) evaluation and summative (outcome) evaluation. Figure 8–1 provides a broad theoretical model to guide research. Formative evaluation should capture the processes that enable teachers to build knowledge during lesson study, such as drawing on important content resources, anticipating student thinking, collecting and discussing data on student thinking and learning, and creating an organized and efficient team process that elicits the ideas of all team members. Changes in lesson plans and in the content of discussion during group meetings provide windows on these issues. Surveys can capture changes in teachers' learning dispositions and experience of professional learning community (for example, teachers' beliefs that instruction can be improved and that they can learn effectively with colleagues). Figure 9–2 (page 105) provides a framework for thinking about mature lesson study, and research papers found at www.lessonresearch.net provide further details on research models and measures.

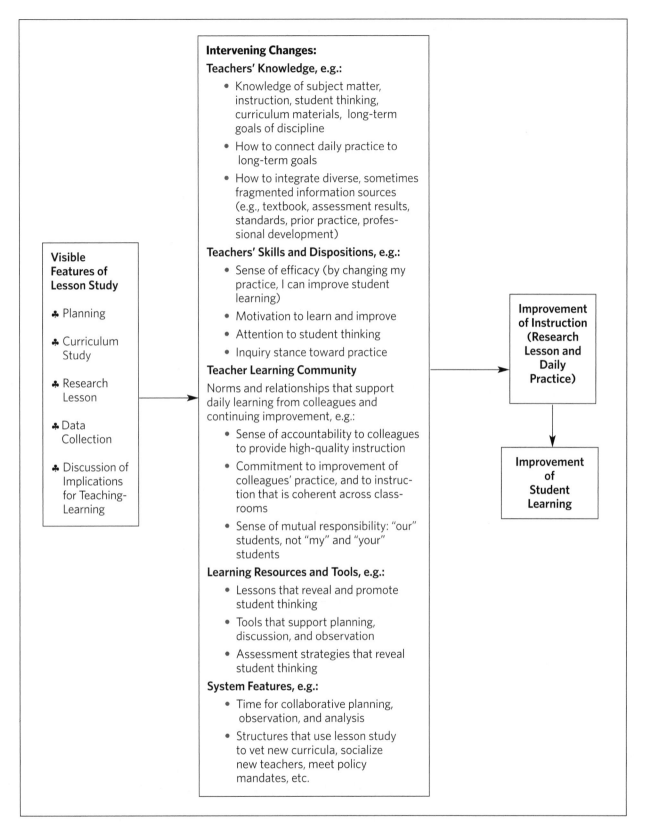

Figure 8-1 Lesson Study Theoretical Model

Common Misconceptions

It's natural to reshape a new idea, such as lesson study, into a familiar mold, such as lesson planning. Over time, educators will no doubt want to adapt lesson study to U.S. circumstances. But at the outset, it's important to understand how lesson study differs from practices that are common in the United States. This section highlights some common misconceptions about lesson study.

1 Lesson Study Is Lesson Planning

Lesson planning is just a small part of lesson study, a larger process that includes formulating long-term goals, studying the content and curriculum, studying student responses to an actual lesson, and revising the approach to instruction. Even the lesson planning itself differs from that familiar to most Americans. In lesson study, teachers' planning focuses on students—on figuring out what students know and how their knowledge can be advanced through well-formulated activities and questions. Teachers anticipate student responses to the lesson activities, and they compare this imagined lesson "drama" to what actually occurs when the lesson is taught. The actual student reactions are used to revamp the lesson plan, and the instructional approach more generally. Only a small fraction of the activities that occur during lesson study are part of traditional U.S. lesson planning.

Our experience suggests that novice lesson study groups sometimes get caught up in planning and teaching the lesson (the middle two parts of the lesson study cycle) and neglect the first and last parts of the cycle—studying the topic and drawing out the implications of the cycle for daily teaching and learning. Make sure the first and last parts of the lesson study cycle receive their due.

The conflation of lesson planning and lesson study may stem in part from translating the Japanese term *jugyou kenkyuu* as *lesson study*. The word *jugyou* (*lesson*) could equally well be translated as *instruction*, and it always refers to *live* instruction, not to a lesson captured on paper. This differs from the English term *lesson*, which is sometimes used interchangeably with *lesson plan*. (For example, you might hand a colleague a piece of paper and say "Please take a look at this lesson," but the term *jugyou* could not be used in this way.) So lesson study is not about lessons on paper but about the whole process of live interaction among students, teacher, and subject matter.

2 Lesson Study Means Writing Original Lessons

Lesson study is not about developing new lessons from scratch. Don't be seduced by the idea of originality. What's important about a research lesson is *not* whether the lesson plan is original, but whether it promotes student learning. It is much better to teach a widely available lesson that really helps students understand the nature of fractions than to teach a fully original lesson that doesn't do the job as well. It is much better to focus on a key topic in your subject area and make small improvements to the current approach than on a peripheral topic where you could do something completely original. Only if teachers build on the best available lessons, focusing on continuous improvement of content that is central to each discipline, will lesson study spark broad improvement.

Lesson study provides a chance to study state-of-the-art approaches and try them in your own setting, refining and adapting them as warranted by student responses. The less writing from scratch your group does, the more time you will have to anticipate student responses and refine the lesson so it works for your students.

Teachers new to lesson study often want to choose or develop a lesson that will "wow" participants—for example, some new or dramatic lesson downloaded from the Internet, or an arcane bit of knowledge that will surprise the teachers. However, these lessons may distract educators from more important collaborative, cumulative work on topics central to the curriculum. Over time, the "wow" in lesson study should come from insights into one's own curriculum and students, not from side trips to exotic places away from the core curriculum (Sisk-Hilton 2009).

3 Lesson Study Produces a Library of Perfect Lessons

Lesson study is not about perfecting lesson plans. It is about creating a system in which teachers actively learn from one another, from the curriculum, and from student thinking. Lesson plans are one important tool in this learning system, as well-designed lesson plans can capture important ideas about subject matter and can promote and reveal student thinking. But lessons are never "perfected" or "finished," just as other kinds of research are not perfected or finished. Even nationally known Japanese educators who teach research lessons in front

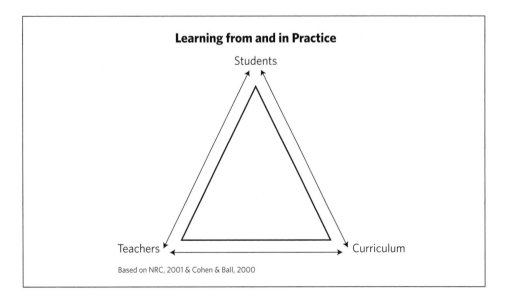

Figure 8–2 Sites for Learning Within Practice

of an audience of a thousand colleagues call these lessons "proposals," with the implication that they can be further improved. Students have different experiences, and the lesson that perfectly connects with the interests of one class may fall flat with another. Teachers differ, and many kinds of knowledge needed to teach effectively can never be captured in a lesson plan.

So a library of perfected lessons is not the goal of lesson study. Lesson study's "product" might be thought of as development of the sites for learning from practice schematically illustrated in Figure 8–2, which shows that teachers have three major sites for learning within their daily practice: through their interaction with curriculum (including standards, teaching manuals, related research, etc.), with colleagues, and with students. In the view of a leading Japanese elementary mathematics educator, Kozo Tsubota, lesson study strengthens each of these three sites of learning and brings them into closer connection with each other, so that, for example, teachers are learning from colleagues' observations and interpretation and implementation of the curriculum, as well as their own.

You may find it interesting to reflect on a lesson study cycle using Figure 8–2 as a lens. Taking the "How Many Seats?" lesson study cycle as an example, we think it is likely that the cycle enhanced participants' capacity to learn from each point of the triangle. For example, with respect to learning from interactions with students, teachers learned that students' counting methods revealed their thinking; after this cycle, teachers became much more deliberate about noticing and recording student counting methods. With respect to curriculum, teachers learned to analyze and question the design of textbook lessons. As Linda commented during the postlesson discussion: "Why did we do this [vertical] pattern? Because it's in there [the textbook]. So that's a really good lesson for us. Just because it's in there . . . is it really the most effective?" With respect to colleagues, teachers improved both the trust and efficiency of their collaborative work, as highlighted in sections such as "Sticking to the process," and in the overall transformation in the group from the beginning to the end of the video.

Formal professional learning rarely happens more than once or twice a month. Every day brings opportunities to learn from practice, so there is great potential in an experience like lesson study that builds capacity to learn from colleagues, students, and curriculum and renders daily practice more educative. Teachers learn not just when they gather for lesson study, but every day, because of the new dispositions, skills, and vision they bring to their daily work with colleagues, students, and curriculum.

An Oakland, California, teacher, reflecting at the end of a lesson study cycle, points to the impact of lesson study on daily practice:

> Lesson study is a very powerful way to develop lessons with student outcome as the primary goal. . . . it makes me think about student learning whenever I plan my daily lessons with our current curriculum. How do I make my lessons sequential for students to totally grasp concepts?

Refining Lessons

We are often asked whether the point of lesson study is to perfect lessons that are then somehow certified and spread. In fact, spread of lessons is largely up to individual teachers who see lessons they like and choose to adapt them for their own use. Professional associations or individual educators often publish volumes of lessons on topics or approaches of current interest. But because the world is diverse and constantly changing, there is no guarantee that a particular lesson is right for all students in all schools, or that it will continue to work well with future students. Lesson study provides a means for teachers to continue to refine lessons so that they can respond effectively to the students in their class *today* (not yesterday). One Japanese teacher, when asked why so many schools adopted research themes related to fostering students' "initiative" and "desire to learn," answered:

> Thirty years ago, Japanese students sat quietly and listened to everything their teachers said, and worked hard to learn whatever the teacher asked. Today's students are different. They are used to TV and video games. They don't have a long attention span. Teachers no longer have such exalted status in Japan. So we need to work hard to interest children in science and every other subject. They aren't interested just because we tell them to be. We must design lessons very well so children want to learn science, and want to pursue questions themselves.

Sound familiar? Because children's lives are changing, lesson study never ends. The "lesson" of lesson study actually refers to the whole of instruction, not just to a single lesson. Is every student learning and growing? Are our materials, instructional techniques, and human relationships fostering our most important long-term goals for students? Even though the lesson study of subtraction with regrouping may end when a good problem is found and a good manipulative designed, other observations made during research lessons (for example, how the students communicated with one another or took initiative) may stimulate the lesson study in a new direction. So the goals and content of lesson study shift over time, but the lesson study itself continues.

4 The Research Lesson Follows a Rigid "Script"

Some educators have the impression that research lessons are rigidly "scripted" and so fail to take advantage of teachers as professionals. Research lessons may be "scripted" in the sense that teachers carefully choose the task or question they will use to promote student thinking, anticipate student responses, and carefully plan how those responses will be built upon and connected during the lesson. A basic idea underlying lesson study is that the content, wording, and presentation of a problem or activity can affect student learning. Another basic idea is the need to anticipate student responses and how they will be used within a lesson. For example, if students use different methods to solve a problem, which methods will be discussed, in what order, and what questions will help students interpret and connect the methods?

When U.S. teachers say that research lessons are "scripted," what may come to mind, however, is a rigid script that teachers read and follow slavishly. This should not be the case. An experienced Japanese educator advises that, for research lessons, teachers should carefully develop the lesson activities and materials and then "forget the teaching materials you spent time making, and instead teach students by looking at each of their faces" (Takahashi 2001, 58). Japanese teachers recognize that a lesson is a "swiftly flowing river" in which many decisions must be made in the moment and that the departures made from a lesson plan often yield important insights for improving a lesson. One Japanese lesson study group is called the Polar Exploration Method. Educators chose this name to call attention to what they see as a similarity between teaching and polar exploration. Both demand expertise, rigorous training, and painstaking advance planning, but at any moment carefully laid plans may need to be altered when an unpredicted Arctic storm—or its classroom equivalent—arises.

5 The Research Lesson Is a Demonstration Lesson or Expert Lesson

Something striking about lesson study is the coequal status of participants. Despite the differences in experience that may occur in a group of teachers, it is assumed that every member will have something important to contribute to lesson study, be it the fresh pair of eyes that someone new to teaching brings or years of experience. One important role of norm setting and facilitation (even if the facilitator rotates each meeting) is to make sure the ideas of each group member are solicited and that each group member feels included. All group members take responsibility for helping to develop the approach and for collection and analysis of data on the students.

Lesson study often adapts nicely to programs of mentoring, coaching, or demonstration lessons, but those situations require some careful thought. For example, if only less experienced teachers teach research lessons, the process may be seen as remedial. If only expert mentors teach research lessons, the idea may take hold that they are perfect models to imitate (or to deride, behind their backs) rather than catalysts to spark study, reflection, and improvement. Akihiko Takahashi often teaches public lessons in front of hundreds of educators. He modestly notes, however, that "the person who teaches the lesson learns the most," reminding us that research lessons are not about providing a perfect model but about continuing to improve one's own teaching and the profession.

A related misconception is thinking about the research lesson as a "show." Especially when conducting a public research lesson or teaching a revised version of a lesson that's been previously taught, it's easy to fall into the trap of treating the research lesson as a performance or show, rather than as a time for your group to learn. Bringing questions and a sense of inquiry to the research lesson is essential. If you no longer have questions about a lesson or aspirations to improve it, the research lesson may end up just a performance rather than a way to build continued learning. Bill Jackson describes one of the big changes in lesson study at Paterson School No. 2 as the shift from focusing on "wow" lessons—those designed to demonstrate some unusual mathematics—to focusing on improvement of regular lessons on central topics.

6 Lesson Study Is Basic Research

The term *lesson study* could equally well be translated as *lesson research* or *instructional research*. Japanese teachers consider lesson study to be research, and they often include in the lesson study concept map a set of "hypotheses" about the changes in instruction that will help students develop in the desired directions. However, lesson study differs in two important ways from most U.S. educational research (and even from some action research).

First, the primary goal of lesson study is not to generate knowledge that *others* will apply. It is to improve instruction for the students in one's own purview, both directly through the research lesson and indirectly through what the participating teachers learn from the process and apply in their own classrooms. The primary goals are always to improve instruction in one's own setting and to document the instruction richly so that others can understand and draw on it if they wish to try something similar. Japanese educators widely share their research lessons, but there is no assumption that what works in one setting will work in exactly the same way in another (as one might assume for a medical drug). Consequently, elements of experimental research such as control groups and observers "blind" to hypotheses are not typical of lesson study. Instead, teachers document what they learned along the way that may be helpful to other teachers, and they scour the classroom for evidence about how students responded to the lesson and what supported or impeded their learning. Lesson study aims to develop the knowledge base for teaching not just by developing knowledge in the form of lesson plans, but also by developing teachers themselves as users and authors of knowledge.

Second, lesson study examines an active improvement effort, not just any idea or question. The question "Why do some children actively participate in science problem solving and others don't?" might guide action research or inquiry. For lesson study, such a question would need to be reformulated as an active intervention. For example, it might be reformulated as: "Does a compelling problem (such as lifting a 100-kilogram sack) encourage all students to participate in science problem solving?" The lesson redesign would then be tried and its impact on student participation studied. The point of lesson study is not to isolate particular variables and study their effects individually, but to practice *all* the qualities thought to comprise good teaching and to do this not just for the research lesson but every day, so colleagues can see the cumulative effects of these practices in one's classroom and school.

In a traditional research model, research is applied to practice. In lesson study, practice *is* research (see Figure 1–1). A physician may diagnose a milk allergy by asking a patient to eliminate milk products and studying what happens. Lesson study's method is similar. For example, teachers notice a problem such as low motivation to study science, make thoughtful changes in their teaching approach, and then carefully observe whether these changes help. Both medical practice and teaching are clinical sciences, primarily concerned with improving clients' well-being and secondarily concerned with generating knowledge to be applied elsewhere.

7 It's All About the Lesson Plan

Although educators new to lesson study sometimes imagine that lesson plans will capture the essence of their lesson study work, student learning and development cannot be assessed by looking at a lesson plan. To say, "It was a good lesson but the students didn't get it" is like saying, "The operation was successful but the patient died."

Several weeks apart, I (Catherine) saw the "same" probability lesson in two U.S. fourth-grade classrooms. The lesson's basic plan is:

- Working in pairs, students draw ten marbles from a large sack of marbles. Each pair of students then predicts the proportion of black and white marbles in the big sack based on their own sample of ten marbles.

- Students look at the data from all the pairs of students and decide whether to revise their own predictions.

- Students discuss whether using the data from all the pairs is likely to lead to a better prediction than just using their own data, and why or why not.

- Students count the marbles in the sack and see whether their individual prediction or the group average came closer to the actual number.

In the fourth-grade classroom where I first saw this lesson, it worked like a charm. Students quickly recognized the power of additional data: "It's just like a baseball average. The more times someone has been at bat, the more accurate the batting average is likely to be." Students in this class were participating in a project that emphasized "a caring community of learners." Through helping to shape class norms and participating in regular class meetings, the students had become very skilled at working together and committed to one another's learning, and their teacher consciously avoided external rewards and competition, preferring to have students operate from a personal commitment to learning.

In a demographically similar classroom just a few miles away, however, the lesson flopped; few students were willing to revise their initial estimates. Very reluctant to admit they were "wrong," students busily defended their initial predictions and refused to use data gathered by other students, justifying their refusal with criticisms like "You probably chose all your marbles from one part of the bag." The elaborate reward system for high achievement and the pervasive sense of competition in this classroom seemed to make it difficult for students to revise their predictions. So even in two nearby, demographically similar classrooms, the "same" lesson met very different fates.

Just as "mistakes are a natural part of learning,"[1] missteps and misconceptions about lesson study are a natural product of efforts to understand lesson study and bring it to life around the world. What next steps will enable us to work through the misunderstandings and build a robust version of lesson study outside Japan? That is the issue addressed in the final chapter.

---

1. Akihiko Takahashi, August 10, 2001, to fifth-grade students in the video "To Open a Cube." Available from www .lessonresearch.net.

chapter 9

Next Steps

Traveler, there is no road; you make your own path as you walk.

—ANTONIO MACHADO

Few things are impossible to diligence and skill. Great works are performed not by strength but by perseverance.

—SAMUEL JOHNSON (EIGHTEENTH-CENTURY ENGLISH SCHOLAR)

The history of education in the United States is filled with innovations that were initially greeted with enthusiasm and later discarded as useless. Lesson study could easily follow the path of so many other once-promising innovations: a rush to implementation; attention to surface features of the innovation rather than its underlying principles; and a premature judgment that the innovation does not work—even though it has not yet been implemented well or for sufficient time. Since the 1999 call for "something like lesson study . . . to be tested seriously in the United States" (Stigler and Hiebert 1999, 131), lesson study has emerged and grown in most regions of the United States and in diverse countries around the world, providing repeated "existence proofs" of its feasibility outside Japan (e.g., Lewis, Perry, and Hurd 2009; Lo, Chik, and Pong 2005). On the other hand, lesson study has fizzled and failed in some settings. What conditions are needed for lesson study to thrive and be effective outside of Japan? We think that the following four challenges will be key to building successful lesson study around the world.

1 Maintain a Spirit of *Hansei* (Self-Critical Reflection)

Lesson study is a simple idea but a complex process. Many of us in the United States have learned to think of new programs as blueprints or recipes: follow the instructions and voila, you are now an expert! Expertise at lesson study does not accrue simply by doing a few cycles, just as expertise at teaching does not accrue just by teaching for a few months. Knowing how to do lesson study well doesn't mean knowing just the surface features like how to conduct, observe, and discuss a research lesson. It means being able to do these things in a way that builds team members' knowledge, instructional skill, and capacity to observe students, and doing it in such a way that everyone will want to *continue* to learn together through lesson study. Something that distinguishes sites that sustain and deepen lesson study is that they are constantly looking for ways to improve it—for example, to build in ways to more forcefully challenge their own content knowledge and beliefs about teaching and to link it to educators' pressing needs. If, after doing several cycles of lesson study, your reaction is "Been there, done that," you probably haven't. Look beyond the recipe, to the underlying purposes outlined in Chapters Six and Eight.

A funny thing happened to me (Catherine) during the months in 1993 when I sat in Japanese elementary classrooms. Woven throughout all of classroom life is *hansei* (pronounced "han-say"), reflection that is often practiced at the end of individual lessons, the school day, the week, the term, and so forth. In *hansei*, students ask themselves questions like "Did I try my very hardest?" "Did I remember all my needed materials for school this week?" and "What areas do I need to improve?" Figure 9–1 shows some student work focused on *hansei*. As students and teachers earnestly reflected on their behavior, it was contagious. I started asking myself whether I had done my very best at my research and what I needed to improve. The habit of self-critical reflection is a key support for lesson study (and for Japanese education more broadly) (Lewis 1995).

The spirit of *hansei*—open, honest reflection focused on improvement of one's shortcomings—is a central value of lesson study. In Japan, research lessons by renowned elementary teachers attract thousands of teachers, but even these teachers do not regard their lessons as models or perfect specimens. Instead, the teachers focus on what can be improved. The logic seems to be that their strengths are already strong, so why should they focus on them? When self-critique and improvement effort are esteemed by others, it creates a very favorable climate for instructional improvement. When introduced at a U.S. event as a "master teacher," Akihiko Takahashi commented that this phrase struck him as odd, since "In Japan, we think of teaching as something that cannot be mastered."

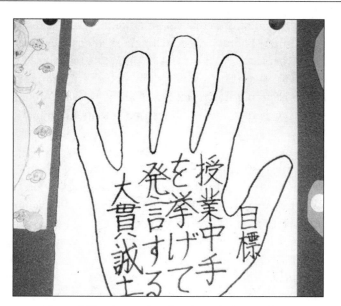

My goal: To raise my hand and speak during class.

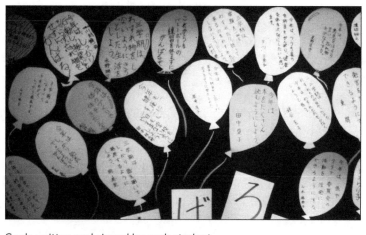

Goals written and signed by each student.

"I'm going to read lots of books this year."

"I'm going to be able to volunteer my ideas often next quarter."

"I'm giong to keep going to volleyball practices and trying my best."

"I'm going to do my club, committee, and chore activities energetically."

"I'm going to try to be healthy this year too, and not miss any school."

Figure 9-1 Examples of hansei (reflection) goals written and illustrated by Japanese elementary students

A study of school improvement in six U.S. districts underlines the importance of offering one's own practice for improvement. One quality that distinguished the successful schools was the willingness of coaches and administrators to share their own instruction and invite critique. Their willingness to open up their own teaching to others and to share their own shortcomings sent a powerful message about the value placed on self-improvement (Solomon et al. 2000). Likewise, by volunteering to teach research lessons, lesson study pioneers can break the ice for others.

At Paterson School No. 2 in Paterson, New Jersey, considered by some an unlikely site for the first lesson study in the United States, Principal Lynn Liptak built lesson study in part through her willingness to put her own practice on the line for scrutiny, by stepping up to the plate to teach a research lesson. She writes, "In lesson study, the principal is not the instructional leader but a lead learner who learns from and with teachers and students" (Liptak 2005, 41).

When asked early in her lesson study career what attitudes were essential to the success of lesson study, Jackie responded:

> That you can always get better at teaching. That you're never at the end of the road.... If you came into [lesson study] and you were [acting] like "I'm the hottest thing out there and I've got all these great ideas and I'll share them with you guys" ... you're not going to get anything out of it.

However wonderful a research lesson is, something can always be improved, if not in the lesson itself, then in some other aspect of student development or classroom climate. An essential value underlying lesson study is to see this gap not as a threat or embarrassment but as a wonderful challenge and a spur to one's fullest development as an educator. Real change takes time and effort and involves making errors along the way. Perfect lessons are as rare as perfect human beings. Lesson study is not a quick fix but a slow, steady means for teachers to improve instruction and to build a school and district culture focused on inquiry and improvement. Perhaps the most surprising threat to lesson study in the United States is the enthusiasts who expect to see perfect research lessons and become discouraged or dismissive when they don't.

The yardstick for measuring the worth of a research lesson is how much teachers learn as they plan, conduct, and discuss the lesson and whether this learning will improve their future instruction and their continued learning from colleagues, students, and curriculum. One can learn a great deal from imperfect lessons, perhaps even more than from highly polished lessons. All nine lessons taught by Japanese and U.S. teachers during the summer 2001 lesson study institute in San Mateo-Foster City encountered challenges, as teachers ran out of time, discovered students' prior knowledge was not as expected, and discovered problems with the manipulatives or questions they had chosen. Yet teachers reported that they learned an enormous amount about teaching and about mathematics during the institute, learning that probably stemmed from seeing the problems their lessons encountered in actual practice and from the chance to discuss these problems with thoughtful colleagues. One lesson instructor, Judith Hitchings, began the discussion of a research lesson she taught by sharing an undated quote from Gordon Moore that appears on the wall of San Jose's Tech Museum of Innovation: "If everything you try works, you are not trying hard enough." Could there be a better motto for lesson study?

2 Keep the Welcome Mat Visible

Sharing one's teaching is an intensely personal, risky activity. Hence members of a lesson study group are likely to develop strong bonds over time. Care must be taken to keep a group open to new members and to fully integrate any newcomer who joins. Although it may be tempting to keep one's lesson study group cozy and unchanged, it is worth remembering the benefits for students when an instructional philosophy begins to appear consistently across classrooms, and this can only happen as groups open up their research lessons to other teachers, as lesson study expands across a school and as teachers see the interconnections of their work to work in other grade levels.

As new members join lesson study, remember the power of assignments that allow team members to support each other's learning. For example, all team members may bring in student work in response to an agreed-upon prompt or investigate how the textbook at their grade level treats a particular topic.

3 Network with Other Lesson Study Groups to Build Regional and National Change

Just as teachers need to learn from each other, sites need to learn from each other. Both lesson study models and instructional models advance when teachers have the opportunity to learn across sites and to see actual lessons that give shared reference points for terms like *problem solving, inquiry learning,* and *reciprocal reading*. Make sure there are ample opportunities for new ideas to come into your lesson study—through collaboration with other lesson study groups, participation in outside networks, invitations for knowledgeable outsiders to observe and comment on your work, or careful study of high-quality curriculum and research. Make sure you visit lesson study at other sites and invite other sites to visit you. "A Closer Look" illuminates the potential of lesson study to catalyze widespread improvement across an entire nation, by ensuring that teachers' knowledge is brought to the work of reforming instruction and textbooks.

The Japanese system of distributed, local, collaborative lesson study work, culminating in public research lessons, enables educators to develop and share the many intertwined types of knowledge needed to enact standards well—knowledge of instructional materials, teaching strategies, student thinking, and content. Such a public proving ground recognizes that translating standards into practice is demanding, important, intellectual work and allows teachers to take initiative in enactment of standards and to bring their important knowledge to bear, rather than experience new policies as something "done to" them. Using lesson study as a public proving ground places students and student thinking at the

A Closer Look: Lesson Study as Public Proving Ground for Standards

In Japan, new national standards cause ripples of activity across the nation, as practitioners and researchers collaborate to bring their ideas to life in public research lessons.

For example, when solar energy was added to the Japanese elementary curriculum, national guidelines specified just the basic objectives for student learning, not the specific teaching methods. Teachers and researchers, working collaboratively in dozens of small groups across the country, studied available research and curriculum (much of it from the United States!). These teams tried out their ideas in a local elementary school, refined their teaching approaches based on student responses, and, after a year or so of experimentation, opened up their instruction in large public research lessons. The tens of thousands of educators, researchers, and policy makers who attended these public research lessons could see and discuss live instruction designed to enact the standards, question the teachers and researchers about the rationale for their choices, scrutinize the entire unit plan and records of student learning across the unit, and offer their own ideas and critiques. Each team focused on the needs of local students, drawing on the work of other teams where useful.

Over the first year or two of public lessons, knowledge about how to teach about solar energy spread rapidly among Japanese educators. Shared knowledge developed about the practical aspects of teaching—for example, which solar toys were inexpensive and made important ideas visible—as well as about the kinds of student thinking to expect, how to handle it, and the subject matter itself. For example, a teacher observing a public research lesson asked about the scientific significance of student strategies, including moving a solar cell closer to a light source, adding a second light source, and using a magnifying class to "concentrate" light:

> I want to know whether the three conditions the children described—"to put the solar cell closer to the light source," "to make the light stronger," and "to gather the light"—would all be considered the same thing by scientists. They don't seem the same to me. But I want to ask the teachers who know science whether scientists would regard them as the same thing.

The Japanese system of distributed, local, collaborative lesson study work, culminating in public research lessons, enables educators to develop and share the many intertwined types of knowledge needed to enact standards well—knowledge of instructional materials, teaching strategies, student thinking, and content.

center of reform and recognizes that the knowledge needed for standards-based instruction cannot all be captured in written documents such as frameworks and teacher manuals. Much knowledge for teaching is embodied in instruction and is spread and refined as teachers watch and discuss practice.

Just Going Through the Motions of Lesson Study

Ideally, lesson study is a means for teachers to answer their pressing questions, investigate new curricula and ideas, recharge their interest in subject matter and in teaching, and help shape the practice of colleagues. But sometimes teachers feel like lesson study is just "going through the motions" designed by someone else. Often this happens when teachers in a lesson study group have not yet had the opportunity to connect lesson study to their own questions and needs. I (Catherine) have inadvertently made this happen by overloading a lesson study group with resources to read. Often it happens when some part of the lesson study cycle doesn't quite function right and comes to feel like an empty ritual. For example, the task used during the lesson may not sufficiently reveal student thinking, so data collection does not yield information of interest. Or there may be too little opportunity to bring in ideas from research or knowledgeable outsiders, leading team members to feel they are just rehashing what they already know. If your group begins to feel as if you are just going through the motions, try to diagnose why and connect your work to questions that are important to you and resources likely to shake up and advance your thinking.

Use Lesson Study to Reshape Policy

Most of this handbook is about using lesson study to reshape *practice*—to establish new, more productive routines in the classroom and in the individual and collaborative work of teachers. In the same way, lesson study offers a powerful tool to reshape *policy* routines. As highlighted in "A Closer Look" (page 102), lesson study provides a way to build, refine, and share classroom-usable knowledge about new standards and to ensure teachers can actively contribute to enactment of policy. In Japan, lesson study shapes textbook content and design, exerting pressure on textbook publishers that is much needed in the United States. For example, in the work leading up to public research lessons in Japan, teachers and researchers together review existing textbooks and research and choose what they believe to be the best approach. Plans written by lesson study groups explain why they chose—and rejected—various textbook approaches. Japanese textbook publishers notice the conclusions emerging from public research lessons and revise textbook contents to reflect what is learned.

In contrast, a researcher describes the process of publishers and state officials crafting curriculum frameworks in the United States: "When people go into a room and come out with solutions, it's typically about money or politics. . . . So the question is, why are people going into that room? What are they after?" (Jon Wiles, quoted in Gewertz 2010, 22). What would happen if "that room" were a classroom? By using classrooms all over a country as the public proving ground to enact, analyze, and refine policies such as common core standards, we can come out with solutions that are *not* about money or politics, but about what and how students are learning.

What Are the Benchmarks of Mature Lesson Study?

Lesson study changes as it matures. Team members internalize key habits of lesson study, such as focusing on student thinking, taking an inquiry stance toward practice, and looking for high-quality resources and research to use in curriculum study.

What changes should you expect to see over time as your lesson study effort matures? The lesson study groups Jackie participated in at Highlands School substantially increased their focus on student thinking over time—from 18 percent of statements during year one meetings to 43 percent of statements during year three meetings.[1] Over the same period, global and fixed-ability evaluations, such as "that was a good lesson" or "he's a low student," declined from 8 percent to fewer than 1 percent of statements during the postlesson discussion, and references to established knowledge sources such as curricula, standards, and research increased from 2 percent to 9 percent of all statements. So, as these Highlands teachers participated in lesson study, they took a less evaluative and more inquiring stance toward practice, using student thinking and research-based sources of knowledge more heavily.

Figure 9–2 provides a reflection tool to examine the development of your lesson study work, based on development of lesson study at sites familiar to us.

If lesson study is to grow, it will be because small groups of U.S. teachers thoughtfully adapt this approach to U.S. settings and share their work with others. These small groups of lesson study pioneers will succeed only if they find the approach genuinely useful; only if it helps them understand students, learning, and subject matter; and only if it helps them teach in ways that are more effective. For their work to grow and spread, administrative and policy supports are likely to be needed.

It will no doubt take time for lesson study in the United States to provide the range of benefits that it does in Japan, where there is a well-developed network of lesson study experiences and publications. But it must provide some benefits, if U.S. educators are to be motivated to do the hard work of bringing lesson study to life. U.S. teachers quoted throughout this volume mention the professional

---

1. Two meetings were transcribed and analyzed from each year: one meeting prior to the research lesson and the postlesson discussion; research details can be found in Perry and Lewis 2010.

Expectations ◇	◇	◇
Initially it was about having great lessons to share.		Now it's about teacher learning

Planning ◇	◇	◇
Initially we consulted only our textbooks and curriculum when designing the lesson.		Now we consult data, research, books, content specialists, and the lessons of other groups. We have built in time to inform our lesson planning by reading and research.

Observations ◇	◇	◇
Initially our observations were about student behavior. Did they follow directions, stay on task, treat each other with respect?		Now we focus on student thinking, uncovering student misconceptions, understanding student strategies. Our data collection is intentional and planned in advance of the lesson, often utilizing data collection forms tailored to the lesson.

Debriefing ◇	◇	◇
Initially our postlesson discussions consisted of reports from each person on what they observed.		Now the discussions are guided by key questions related to the goals of the lesson, and we discuss the implications for future instructions.

Balance ◇	◇	◇
Initially we spent most of our time planning the lesson, so that when we taught it, the lesson felt like the grand finale!		Now the cycle is more balanced; we often teach a "dirty" lesson first to clarify our goals and gather data. We spend time after the research lesson reflecting on what we have learned and outlining our conclusions, often revising and further investigating the lesson.

Balance ◇	◇	◇
Initially we relied on old habits to manage our meetings.		Now we use shared protocols for rotating group roles, establishing group norms, setting agendas, and keeping meeting notes.

Figure 9-2 How Has Our Lesson Study Changed?

satisfactions of connecting one's daily practice to long-term goals and the intellectual satisfaction of solving challenging problems related to student learning. But perhaps the most important motivator for teachers conducting lesson study is their feeling of increased efficacy in the classroom. Harlem Village Academy educator Nick Timpone, in response to a questionnaire in January 2001, reflected:

> Lesson study has made me much more aware of the need to engage the students in each and every lesson. How can I pique their interest? How can I vary my style of teaching? Lesson study has made me a more reflective and patient teacher. I teach with less brute force.

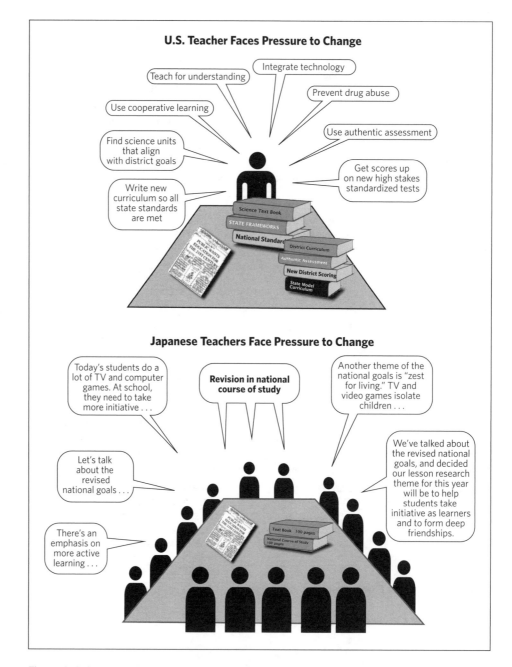

Figure 9-3 Pressure on Japanese and U.S. Teachers

Lesson study should also provide a welcome force of coherence for teachers, supporting them as they make sense of reforms and translate them into classroom practice. As pictured in Figure 9–3, U.S. teachers in many settings face myriad, sometimes contradictory, reforms, often without adequate time or an established process to make sense of these reforms. Although the Japanese teachers pictured in Figure 9–3 also face tremendous pressure to change (rapid change seems to be a fact of postindustrial society), they face fewer, more coherent demands, and they face them together, with support from a frugal, coherent curriculum and standards. Lesson study provides a systematic venue for Japanese teachers to discuss, try out, and rethink Japan's reform goals such as enabling students to "take initiative as learners" and "learn with desire." U.S. teachers do not need one more thing on their already overfilled plates. For lesson study to succeed, U.S. teachers must find that it is not "one more thing," but, instead, a process that enables them to make sense of the things already on their plates.

One cannot overestimate the importance of the lesson study pioneers who have emerged across the United States and who have been doing this work for more than a decade. If lesson study thrives in the United States, it will be because these teachers, and others who join them, do the sustained, challenging, thoughtful work of adapting lesson study to U.S. circumstances and because they persist in making this approach genuinely useful to themselves and to other teachers. It will be because they are willing to share their learning with others, as have teachers across North America and around the world who have courageously opened up their research lessons to educators from outside their schools, and whose eager students remind us all of the importance of this work. Bill Jackson, one of the originators of the Paterson School No. 2 lesson study effort, writes:

> I feel that the biggest mistake we can make when pitching lesson study to U.S. teachers is to tell them that it is easy and painless. It is hard and possibly painful and they should prepare for it. The rewards, however, are fantastic. Real, concrete, observable improvement occurs in teaching.

Our lesson study pioneers will need to be brave enough to challenge the norms of privacy and isolation that pervade so many schools and to take on work that is both intellectually and interpersonally demanding. When we first undertook lesson study, we were often told that it wouldn't work within U.S. culture. But our many lesson study colleagues have powerfully demonstrated that school culture is created by human beings and can be changed by them. Will you join us?

Lesson Plan Example: "How to Open a Cube"

Mathematics Lesson Plan (for Grade 5)

For the lesson on Friday, August 10, 2001, at Brewer Island School, San Mateo, California.
Instructor: Akihiko Takahashi.

1. Title of the lesson: "How Many Edges Do I Need to Cut to Open a Cube?"
2. Goals
   a. Deepen students' understanding of three-dimensional geometric objects through problem-solving activities.
   b. Help students become good problem solvers by providing a challenging open-ended problem.
      i.   Encourage students to use their existing knowledge to solve a challenging problem.
      ii. Encourage students to find common properties and relationships among various patterns by comparing peers' solutions to find a solution to the problem.
      iii. Encourage students to consider their solutions from a different perspective, so that they can make reasoned conjectures.
   c. Provide students with opportunities to find the importance of working with peers to deepen their understanding of mathematics.
3. Relationship of the lesson to the *Mathematics Content Standards for California Public Schools K–Grade 12.*

Grade 2
Students identify and describe the attributes (the number and shape of faces, edges, and vertices) of common figures in the plane and of common objects in space (including cube, rectangular prism, sphere, and pyramid).

Grade 3
Identify, describe, and classify common three-dimensional geometric objects (including cube, rectangular solid, sphere, prism, pyramid, cone, cylinder). Identify common solid objects that are the components needed to make a more complex solid object.

Grade 4
Visualize, describe, and make models of geometric solids in terms of the number and shape of faces, edges, and vertices; interpret two-dimensional representations of three-dimensional objects; and draw patterns (of faces) for a solid that, when cut and folded, will make a model of the solid.

THIS PROBLEM-SOLVING LESSON

Grade 5
Construct a cube and rectangular box from two-dimensional patterns and use those patterns to compute the surface area for those objects. Visualize and draw two-dimensional views of three-dimensional objects made from rectangular solids.

4. Instruction of the lesson. The lesson is designed to provide students with an opportunity to use their understanding of geometric objects, developed though previous mathematics lessons, to solve a problem that students otherwise might not be able to solve, because no routine path is apparent.

According to the *Mathematics Content Standards for California Public Schools K–Grade 12*, in grade 3 students are introduced to the cube as one common three-dimensional geometric object. In grade 4, students experience visualizing, describing, and making models of geometric solids. Through these learning experiences, students develop their understanding of basic geometric solids such as the cube. These experiences include:

- describing a geometric solid in terms of the number of faces, edges, and vertices
- interpreting two-dimensional representations of three-dimensional objects
- drawing patterns of faces for a solid that, when cut and folded, will make a model of the solid

In today's lesson, students are expected to solve the following problem using these learning experiences.

> How many edges of a cube do you need to cut to open a cube completely and make a net? Find the least number of edges that need to be cut.

One reason I have chosen this problem is that it provides students with an opportunity to extend their problem-solving strategies. To solve this problem, first students may actually cut and open cube models so that they can find how many edges they need to cut to open the cube. Next, students are expected to establish a conjecture that the least number of edges might be seven; however, the answer cannot be finalized by opening only one or two cube models. Because there are eleven different ways to open a cube by cutting seven edges, which means there are eleven different patterns of nets, students will have the opportunity to compare and discuss with peers to find general properties and relationships among the eleven nets, and this will lead students to establish a conjecture. This series of activities will help students develop their problem-solving strategies. Students are expected to develop the following strategies described in the *Mathematics Content Standards for California Public Schools Grade 5*:

- Use a variety of methods, such as words, numbers, symbols, charts, graphs, tables, diagrams, and models, to explain mathematical reasoning (Mathematical Reasoning 2.3).
- Express the solution clearly and logically by using the appropriate mathematical notation and terms and clear language; support solutions with evidence in both verbal and symbolic work (Mathematical Reasoning 2.4).

This problem also provides students with an opportunity to use what they have learned through the end of grade 4. This lesson will play an important role in bridging students' previous understanding of the material with the California Standards goal for the new grade level. Because students will be expected to construct cubes and rectangular boxes from two-dimensional patterns and use the patterns to compute the surface areas of these objects in grade 5, this problem will not only establish an opportunity to develop students' problem-solving strategies but also make a connection from the contents that students have learned in prior years to the new content they will learn in grade 5.

APPENDIX A – LESSON PLAN EXAMPLE: "HOW TO OPEN A CUBE"

5. Lesson procedure

LEARNING ACTIVITIES TEACHER'S QUESTIONS AND EXPECTED STUDENT REACTIONS	TEACHER'S SUPPORT	POINTS OF EVALUATION
1. Introduction to the Problem	Ask students to tell what they have learned about cube by showing a model of cube.	Do the students recall the properties of cube?
How many edges of a cube do you need to cut in order to open a cube completely and make a net? Find the least number of edges that need to be cut.		
	Show students how to cut and open a cube by using a model if necessary.	Do students understand the problem?
2. Individual Problem Solving Find how many edges need to be cut to open a cube by opening several cube models.	Encourage students to find as many different ways to open a cube as possible.	Does each student find more than two ways to open a cube?
3. Comparing and Discussing (1) Help students form a conjecture that the least number of edges might be seven. (2) Facilitate students' discussion about their conjecture. Five edges must remain attached in order to make a cube turn into a two-dimensional pattern from a cube. If six edges remain attached, a cube cannot turn into a two-dimensional pattern. (3) Help students discover a relationship between the number of edges that a cube has and the number of edges that connect six faces in each net.	Help students to discover that all eleven nets share common properties: • Each net has six faces. • Six faces are connected by five edges. • Seven edges should be cut to open a cube and to make a net. 12 [number of edges of a cube] – 5 [number of the edges remaining attached after opening a cube] = 7 [number of edges to be cut]	Does each student find out that all the eleven nets share common properties?
4. Find the solution to the problem Help students understand that they need to cut at least seven edges in order to open a cube.		
5. Summing up (1) Using blackboard writing, review what students learned through the lesson. (2) Ask students to write a journal entry of what they learned through the lesson.		

6. Evaluation

a. Were the students able to find several ways to open a cube and find out how many edges needed to be cut?

b. Were the students able to compare the eleven patterns of nets and find general properties and relationships among the nets to establish a conjecture?

c. Were students able to review what they learned through the lesson and write about it in their journal?

Plan for organizing the blackboard

How many edges of a cube do you need to cut in order to open a cube completely?
Find the least number of edges needed to be cut.

What do you know about a cube?

The number of edges
The number of faces
The number of vertices

What do you want to do in order to solve the problem?

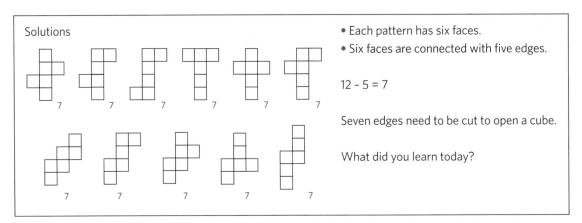

Solutions

7   7   7   7   7   7

7   7   7   7   7

• Each pattern has six faces.
• Six faces are connected with five edges.

12 – 5 = 7

Seven edges need to be cut to open a cube.

What did you learn today?

Aug. 10, 2001, by Akihiko Takahashi for Lesson Study Summer Workshop

"How Many Seats?" Viewing Guide

This guide suggests a process for using the DVD "How Many Seats?" to become acquainted with lesson study.

Before viewing the DVD, take a moment to consider the following three questions and to jot down your thoughts. These are meant to be quick warm-up questions.

1. What do you believe are the characteristics of good professional learning? Please make a list. (If working with colleagues, share and discuss your lists.)

2. What do you expect are the challenges and benefits of lesson study, based on what you know now?

3. What are some burning issues (challenges in your teaching) you would like to investigate with your colleagues?

4. Before watching the DVD, spend a few minutes solving the following mathematical task that will be assigned to students, so you can understand teachers' and students' conversations about the task. After solving it individually, share and discuss strategies if you are working with colleagues.

> How many seats can fit around a row of triangle tables arranged in a row as shown?
>
> How many seats for three triangle tables? Five? *X*?

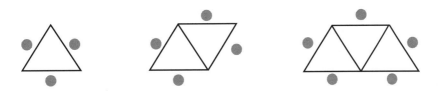

DVD Segment 1: Planning and Study

5. Observe video clip, Planning and Study, all three parts: You will see teachers pick a lesson, reflect on their team's working processes, and investigate the mathematics content. While watching the video, note:
   - how the group's work is similar to or different from your usual experiences of lesson planning and collaboration
   - any opportunities you see for teachers to build their knowledge of mathematics or other professional qualities

Notice that team members:

- start with an existing lesson—they do not develop a lesson from scratch
- monitor group norms and work to uphold them
- rotate roles (e.g., facilitator and recorder)
- spend time doing the mathematical task they will have students do and anticipate student thinking
- work to deepen their own content knowledge

DVD Segment 2: First Teaching

6. In video clip 2, you will observe the first research lesson. As you watch this portion, imagine that you are in the room observing the students, and collect as much as data as you can on their understanding of the plus-two pattern and how the pattern grows.

7. After viewing the video, review the data you collected (sharing with a partner if available) to identify what your data reveal about student understanding. What data would you want to share in the postlesson discussion? What questions would you ask?

DVD Segment 3: First Postlesson Discussion

8. Watch the video clip of the postlesson discussion.

9. Decide what changes you would make to the lesson, based on the lesson segments you observed and the ideas raised during the postlesson discussion. (Discuss this as a group if you are watching the video with others.)

10. The lesson study team made the following revisions to the lesson:
    - eliminated the worksheet
    - gave each student a three-by-five card with a unique number of tables written on the left half; on the right half, the students filled in the number of seats for that number of tables; students then shared their findings with their group and wrote about the patterns
    - early in the lesson, selected students presented to the class their strategies for counting the number of seats

    What do you predict students will do the same or differently in the next lesson?

DVD Segment 4: Second Teaching

11. Watch the video clip "Second Teaching," the second research lesson. Observe and make notes on students, recording as much information as you can about:
    - students' understanding of the plus-two pattern and how the pattern grows

    If viewing the video with colleagues, share and discuss the data on student understanding you recorded.

DVD Segment 5: Second Postlesson Discussion and Segment 6: Final Reflection

12. Watch video clips 5 and 6.

13. How do you think the future practice of these teachers might be affected by their participation in this lesson study cycle?

14. Revisit your list of characteristics of good professional learning. How does the lesson study shown in this video fit with or conflict with your ideas about good professional learning?

15. During which part of the lesson study process do you feel you would need the most support?

Writing Teaching-Learning Plan for Grade 3

Date: January 30, 2006, and February 15, 2006

Site: Highlands School

Planning Team: Monika Hastings, Tami Wong, Lisa Brown, Linette Griffith, Jane Danbold, Suzi Riley, Jackie Hurd

Instructors: Jackie Hurd and Tami Wong

1. Title of Lesson: Don't hold back that feeling!

2. Goals of the Lesson

- Students will experiment with adding emotion to a notebook entry, bringing a character more to life and pulling the reader into the story by utilizing one of the strategies they identified in a previous lesson from other text.

- Students will share their compulsory "try it" of adding emotion with a partner.

- Students will demonstrate Active Listening during the minilesson and during their partner work and Perseverance during their writing block.

3. Relationship of the Lesson to Standards

Grade 1
Noyce Grade 1 Writing Standard   In some cases, begin to recount not just events but also reactions, signaled by phrases like "I wondered," "I noticed," "I thought," or "I said to myself," California Content Standards 1.0 Writing Strategies Students write clear and coherent sentences and paragraphs that develop a central idea. Their writing shows they consider the audience and purpose. Students progress through the stages of the writing process (e.g., prewriting, drafting, revising, editing successive versions).

Grade 2

Noyce Grade 2 Writing Standard

    Develop internal events as well as external ones; for example, the child may tell not only what happened to a character but what the character wondered, remembered, hoped.

California Content Standards

2.1 Write brief narratives based on their experiences:

1. Move through a logical sequence of events.
2. Describe the setting, characters, objects, and events in detail.

Grade 3

Noyce Grade 3 Narrative Writing Standard

    Develop a character, often by providing motivation for action and having the character solve the problem. Adds reflective comments (especially in autobiographical narrative). *Uses story strategies that build pace and tension, uses dialog, and creates a believable world with precise choice of detail.*

California Content Standards

2.1 Write narratives:

1. Provide a context within which an action takes place.
2. Include well-chosen details to develop the plot.
3. Provide insight into why the selected incident is memorable.

Grade 4

Noyce Grade 4 Narrative Writing Standard

    Include sensory details and concrete language to develop plot and character. Use a range of appropriate strategies such as dialog and tension or suspense.

California Content Standards

2.1 Write narratives:

1. Relate ideas, observations, or recollections of an event or experience.
2. Provide a context to enable the reader to imagine the world of the event or experience.
3. Use concrete sensory details.
4. Provide insight into why the selected event or experience is memorable.

4. Rationale

What do students already understand about this topic? What more do we want them to understand? What thinking have we done that guided our decisions?

We began our work this year wanting to investigate strategies that would have the greatest impact on helping our SED (socioeconomically disadvantaged) students attain performance at grade-level standards. At our first schoolwide meeting we "jigsawed" the following articles: "Strategies That Close the Gap" by Larry Bell, "How Student Progress Monitoring Improves Instruction" by Nancy Safer and Steve Fleischman, and "High-Quality Teaching and Instruction" by Learning Point Associates. Some of the insights we gained and wanted to build upon in our research this year include:

- The knowledge with which students come to school affects their ability to learn new knowledge. SED students have comparatively fewer experiences to build upon in acquiring new academic knowledge and so we must provide rich experiences at school so that they can more easily make new connections.

- It is important to review with students about their daily learning and provide opportunities for them to articulate and reflect on what they learn.

- It should be made clear how new learning is connected to prior learning. Reviewing and referring to previous units builds the seeds for long-term memory.

- Inquiry-based instruction is an effective strategy for drawing out students' current assumptions and using them as the building blocks for the construction of new knowledge.

We identified the strategy of teacher modeling of her own writing as well as using good models of writing to help improve student writing. We believe that these strategies will help to build rich experiences for students, frequently exposing them to quality literature, and building connections between other authors' writing and their writing. Our goal is: "We will investigate how to effectively use teacher modeling of her own writing and exemplary samples of student and authors' text to improve student narrative writing."

We are still developing an understanding of the distinction between *modeling* as the act of the teacher actually thinking aloud and/or writing a piece in front of students and the act of *using models* or examples of writing to show something to students. We may look more closely at each in subsequent lessons to clarify when each strategy is more appropriately used for the greatest impact on students.

We reviewed student work samples from our SED students in grades 1–4 and characterized them as: having limited vocabulary, needing guidance in conventions and grammar, looking more like a list of ideas, often poorly organized and reading like a "bed-to-bed" story. We decided to have each teacher in our group do an on-demand writing assessment of her students. We scored these samples at a following meeting and compared them to successful anchor papers of students performing at grade-level standard.

Our goal for this year is that when we score students' samples again at the end of the year, our SED students are able to perform at grade-level standard. We will identify the standards that are in place from previous grades for students who are not yet at grade-level standard, to help clarify the appropriate intervention strategies.

While considering this baseline data we collected on our students and the needs it revealed we reviewed the NCEE writing standards for grades K–5. We wanted to identify a standard to focus on in our research lesson that would be helpful for each of the first- through fourth-grade teachers in our group. We decided to focus on teaching the strategy of showing emotion in a piece of writing.

We decided to plan our research lesson for a third-grade classroom where students are already engaged in a unit on writing Narrative Memoir. The teacher has been using the NCEE genre study lessons and *Craft Lessons* by Ralph Fletcher and Joann Portalupi. In these curriculum materials lesson topics or writing strategies are addressed in one lesson. This contributed to a misconception of teachers that their students should be showing evidence of utilizing the strategy after one lesson. It was pointed out by our content coaches that several lessons on a strategy are often needed for students to successfully internalize the strategy.

As we did not know of a preexisting lesson for teaching the strategy of showing emotion in writing we designed a lesson building upon the work the students were already doing on Narrative Memoir. In previous lessons the third graders had read a piece of student writing, "When I Lost My Stuffed Seal" and *My Rotten Redheaded Older Brother*, by Patricia Polacco and identified the characteristics of a narrative memoir. We decided to use these two models again to introduce the idea of how an author shows emotion in writing.

In the first lesson the teacher read aloud *My Rotten Redheaded Older Brother* and asked students to stop her as they noticed ways the author was showing emotion. The students identified the strategies of use of dialogue, emotional words, and physical description of how a character is feeling. In the second lesson the students highlighted with a partner where the author of "When I Lost My Stuffed Seal" showed emotion in writing. The students were able to again identify places where the author used emotional words, dialogue, and physical description to reveal emotion and for the most part highlighted appropriate places. However, students had difficulty labeling or naming these strategies or comparing them to the strategies in the previous lesson. Students also highlighted places in the story where the author used sound effects to enhance the setting. Although it did not contribute to showing emotion in the piece, students probably highlighted it because it was very successful at capturing their attention. In these two lessons the *use of models* rather than *modeling* was the strategy employed.

In this research lesson the teacher will use the strategy of modeling. She will think aloud while revising her writing by adding a physical description of emotion to a piece previously shared with students. Students will be asked to "try it" in their writing notebooks and share their "try it" at the end of the period.

APPENDIX C – LESSON PLAN FOR GRADE 3

5. Lesson Description

STUDENT ACTIVITIES	ANTICIPATED STUDENT RESPONSES	POINTS OF EVALUATION
1. Introduction: Minilesson Last week we took a look at "When I Lost My Stuffed Seal" and underlined all the places where the author showed emotion. We identified four strategies that author used, (review strategies). I'm going to try to use one of those strategies in my story about playing Apples to Apples with my family. I thought adding more emotion could make this piece more interesting for the reader. I'm going to use the strategy of adding physical description of emotion.	Most students will be listening and following along as the teacher models revising her writing.	
Teacher models thinking aloud about where to add physical description of emotion and makes changes to the writing example.	Some students may try to offer suggestions of things to add to her writing, because they are always trying to be the boss.	
Turn and Talk—How did my adding a physical description of my emotion to the story make it better for you as a reader?		Are students able to see the impact this had on the story?
Teacher will share a few of the comments overheard with the whole group.	"It helped me understand better how you were feeling."	
Today I'd like you to try this strategy of adding a physical description of the emotion to see if you can add more emotion to a piece in your notebook.	"I could tell how happy you felt now." "It made the story more interesting."	
When you go back to your desk, I'd like you to pick a piece from your notebook where you can try this strategy. I'll give you a green sticky note to stick on the page where you tried it, because at the end of our writing time today you will have a chance to share where you tried it with a partner and we will share some with the whole class. After you have tried this strategy of adding emotion to one piece you can continue with whatever you were working on in your notebook.		

(continues)

STUDENT ACTIVITIES	ANTICIPATED STUDENT RESPONSES	POINTS OF EVALUATION
2. Writing Block Students will return to their seats and do the compulsory "try it" of adding emotion to one piece in their notebooks. They will then continue work in their writers' notebooks.	Some students may have difficulty finding a place to add emotion. Some students may be paralyzed because they "don't know what to write about." Some students may want to try a different strategy, like using dialogue to show emotion. Some students may add in physical description that is not related to emotion.	Were students able to add emotion by using the strategy of adding a physical description? Were their revisions beneficial to the story?
3. Summing Up 10 minutes before the end of the session students will be asked to finish the sentence or idea they are working on. They then will be asked to find their "try it" of adding emotion to their writing and share it with their partner. Volunteers, or teacher-selected volunteers, will then have an opportunity to read a few to the whole class from the Author's Chair.	Hopefully there will be one or two student examples to share with the whole class.	Do students see the value of these changes to their writing?

6. **What do we want to look for during the lesson observation?**

How long will it take them to find the place to revise? How do they seem to find the place to revise? How long to they spend revising? Do they use the strategy in more than one place?

Is there a correlation between these and the effectiveness of their revision? Do students seem proud or excited about being able to use this new strategy?

7. Conclusions

We examined the importance of teacher modeling and realized it is an important teacher strategy to be used thoughtfully. Teacher thinking aloud while writing makes the writing process explicit for students. It was important for teachers to become writers so they can better understand the struggles of the students as writers.

We were surprised that second graders were able to grasp the concept of physical description, which is a third-grade concept or higher. The content was more accessible to the EL/SED students than we anticipated; their success exceeded our expectations.

Rituals, routines, procedures for writers' workshop support the SED students.

By examining the Noyce and California Standards we saw the emphasis on narrative writing across the grades.

Utilizing a preassessment with students was helpful in determining how to target the lesson. The assessment was repeated during and after the unit.

WWS has a built-in differentiation strategy of conferencing with SED students immediately after the minilesson. This allowed immediate feedback and direction for our targeted students.

Oral rehearsals, oral storytelling helped students be ready for writing as well as students acting out their feelings. Another support was the use of a visual aid (Feelings Chart).

Holding the minilesson to ten minutes also supported the SED students in keeping a keen focus on what it is the target of the lesson; repeating the targeted language repeatedly during the lesson was also helpful.

Clear and explicit language supported SED students.

Utilizing an anchor during the minilesson gives the students a common reference for that concept over time.

I whent to Mexico over summer brake to visit my familly and friends. I had a long trip. I also went alown on the plane. When I gotithere evrebody was waiting for me. My granpa and granma touch me were they plant seeds I saw a big fat seery lithery snak and my granpa holded the snake I vas scerd, but then he got a littler snake. I holded it too. Then I saw a Salummander and I Ceepad it as a pet. The they touck me to the super market I bot a big ball it had the whole contry of Mexico it was So So So prity I also whent to the beach I made a big sandy Sand casel with a flag on the top it was the colors of Mexico which are red, white, and green. My granpa made a a sandy sandman he used shells for the eyes and left over nut shells for the nose and I did the mouth with a lot of prity shells. then we whent swimmig in the beach it was realy fun my grama gave me the prityest shell.

Classroom Profile

Third-Grade Narrative

STANDARDS Student Name	Orients the reader (sets time, place, and situation)	Develops plot, usually problem/ solution	Develops character using motivation	Uses story strategies	Concludes story believably	Adds reflective comments (especially in autobiographical narrative)

Sample First Meeting Agenda for Groups New to Lesson Study

TIME (MIN.)	AGENDA ITEM
5	**Choose Roles (See Appendix F)**
	Agree on roles and assign roles for today's meeting. Use roles that have worked for you in the past, or roles such as: • facilitator • two note takers (one electronic, one for writing in public view) • timekeeper Rotate roles each meeting, and add roles as needed (e.g., researcher to track down materials, lesson plan recorder to update and circulate research lesson plan, convener to send out reminders and arrange room and refreshments).
15–20	**Develop Group Norms**
	Develop norms (ground rules) and identify a norm to monitor at today's meeting. A protocol for this can be found in Appendix G.
45–70	**Become Familiar with Lesson Study**
	Examine your ideas about professional development (10 min.). In your view, what are the characteristics of effective professional development? Write lists individually and then share with the group.
	Build shared understanding of lesson study (20–40 min.). Using guide, in Appendix B, observe video "How Many Seats?" or read "A Deeper Look at Lesson Study" if you prefer. If meeting time is limited, you can do this ahead of time in preparation for the meeting. Discuss: What are the key characteristics of lesson study?
	Revisit ideas about effective professional development (10 min.). How do characteristics of lesson study fit/not fit with ideas about effective professional development generated by this group?
	Elicit concerns about lesson study (5–10 min.).
10–20	**Consider Your Long-Term Goals and "Research Theme" (See Appendix J)**
5–10	**Build a Timeline for the Lesson Study Cycle and Set a Schedule**
10	**Meeting Review and Reflection** Summarize decisions, any assignments, build tentative agenda for next meeting.
	Reflect on norm(s) selected to monitor today: Did we uphold norm(s)? What do we need to do differently next meeting?

Lesson Study Group Roles

Facilitator: Keeps the conversation moving and fair. Involves all participants. Follows an agreed-upon agenda.

Note Taker: Takes the minutes of the meeting, copies and distributes them to members for review before the next meeting.

Recorder: Records on chart paper, where all can see, important decisions of the group (helpful when brainstorming goals and planning the lesson design).

Typist: Types up the lesson plan or any other documents as needed.

Liaison/Convener: Communicates with any outsiders for the group, requests subs, reminds members of meeting dates, times, and places, arranges room and refreshments.

Member: Supports others in their roles, actively contributes to the meeting's running smoothly.

Guide to Developing Group Norms

What would make this lesson study group a supportive and productive site for your learning?

- Jot down a list of characteristics that are important to you. (It may help to think about characteristics of groups that have functioned well—or poorly—to support your professional learning in the past.) You may want to consider some general norms (such as listening and taking responsibility) and some that have been identified as especially important to supporting learning of academic content, such as expressing agreement/disagreement and explaining your thinking.

- As a group, share and discuss the ideas generated by each member, taking particular care to identify and discuss any possible contradictions. For example, if one group member asks for "safe" and another for "challenging my thinking," talk about how both can be honored.

- Synthesize members' ideas to a group list of about five key norms you all support.

- Record the norms for future reference.

- At the beginning of each meeting, choose one norm to monitor that day. At the end of your meeting, discuss whether you upheld it and what can be improved.

Highlands School Meeting Agenda

The Challenge of Proficiency for Every Child (Session 2)

Bring sample work from your target students to the meeting—see starred item.

October 11, 2005

Goals for Today's Meeting

1. Identify a content area to work in.
2. Identify the two low socioeconomic status (SES) students from each class who will be the focus of your work.
3. Determine your research goal that will address increasing achievement for socioeconomically disadvantaged (SED) students.
4. Develop a timeline for the work this year.

---

15 min.

Get Organized

- Select a facilitator and recorder for this meeting.
- Review your lesson study group norms and identify one to monitor today's meeting.
- Review your minutes from your last meeting.

15 min.

Schoolwide Goal

The following is a synthesis of ideas shared at our first sessions. Does it capture your sense of the broad school goal that we discussed? Do you have any suggested changes?

How can we improve our use of effective Integrated Thematic Instruction (ITI) and differentiation strategies to help all students, and in particular our SED students, access their full potential and improve their performance relative to grade-level standards?

20 min.

Narrow the Focus of Your Work

We are going to pick up at the halfway point of our last meeting agenda, as most folks probably only got this far. Please adjust based on how far your team progressed at your last meeting.

- Identify two SED students you would like to focus on in your classroom this year. You will monitor these students' progress toward grade-level standards in your selected content area.

- Share some sample work by your identified students in the content area that your group has selected. After reviewing the samples of student work from each student, identify some common areas of concern across this group of students. Sketch a picture of the general most pressing needs of these students.
- What are your goals for these students? Describe as specifically as possible at this point in the year examples of work you would like your students to be able to do by the end of the year.

Formalize Your Research Question

- Are you considering any changes in the content area(s) that your group selected at your previous meeting?
- What teaching/learning strategies would you like to investigate this year? What is your hypothesis about how this strategy will help students more effectively access their potential and increase their performance?
- Write up your question or hypothesis for your lesson study representative to share with representatives from our other lesson study teams.

Build a Plan to Gather Some Data—Make a Timeline

30 min.

Last year, several groups taught an initial research lesson for the purposes of gathering baseline data. This was intended to be a routine lesson, taught every year, that would not require group planning (a "dirty lesson"). The purpose in doing this again would be to give you an opportunity to gather baseline data on the differentiation strategies you are already using targeted to SED students. Some groups found this step very helpful in fine-tuning the goals of their work for the year.

We would like to ask you to develop a timeline for your work this year. If possible, please identify the dates you would like to teach your first and second research lessons. There is a tremendous challenge with getting access numbers for subs this year, so the sooner we have dates, the better our chances of obtaining subs.

Using the Highlands Staff Meeting Schedule, devise a timeline for your work. Working backward, May 16 will be our schoolwide meeting to share our work. You probably want to save April 25 for writing up your conclusions and preparing your presentation. You therefore may want to plan for your first research lesson (the routine lesson) in November and your second planned lesson for March.

Will you be willing to teach your research lesson on a Wednesday afternoon so that more staff members can attend?

Please consider if there are any additional resources you would like to request this year. Would you like to invite a literacy or Gifted and Talented Education (GATE) coach to one of your meetings? Will you need any help finding additional research or articles to help inform your work?

Reflect on This Lesson Study Session

10 min.

- Summarize decisions that were made during this meeting. Are there any assignments for the next meeting?
- Record ideas for things you would like to accomplish at the next meeting.
- Give each member an opportunity to reflect on how well you practiced the norms you agreed upon.

First Lesson Study Team Representative meeting, Wednesday, Nov. 9, 3:15, Staff Room. Please bring your timelines.

Sample Protocols to Begin and End Each Lesson Study Meeting

Opening Protocol

- Choose group roles (recorder, etc.) (see Appendix F).
- Select a norm to monitor and briefly share ideas about what this norm looks like.
- Review the desired outcomes or research theme for this year's work.
- Review the minutes from the last meeting.
- Review and revise today's agenda as needed.

[Agenda content will vary.]

Closing Protocol

- Review key decisions made during the meeting.
- Agree upon assignments to be done by the next meeting and an agenda for the next meeting.
- Reflect on the norm selected to monitor today. Allow each member to comment on how they did in respecting the norm.

Choosing a Research Theme

Think about the students you serve. Jot down your ideas about each item before reading the next item.

Your Ideals

Ideally, what qualities would you like these students to have five to ten years from now (or alternately, when they graduate your institution)?

The Actual

List their qualities now.

The Gap

Compare the ideal and the actual. What are the gaps that you would most like to address as an educator?

The Research Theme (The Goal, Research Focus, or Main Aim of Lesson Study)

By comparing the ideal and actual student qualities, select a focus for your lesson study. State *positively* the ideal student qualities you choose to work on. For example, teachers in a Japanese school serving a low-income, diverse community that had historically been subjected to discrimination chose the following goal:

> For students to develop fundamental academic skills that will guarantee their advancement and a rich sensibility about human rights.

Your Research Theme _____

Mathematics Teaching-Learning Plan

Plan to Guide Learning in Mathematics

(Second Public Teaching of Research Lesson)

November 27, 1998
Students: fifth-grade, class B; thirty-six students (seventeen boys, nineteen girls)
Instructors: Yumiko Tanaka and Michiko Honma

Research Theme: To Nurture Children with Rich Spirits Who Continue to Learn

1. Unit: Circles and Regular Polygons

2. About the Unit

Circles are taught in third grade and the concept and properties of polygons are taught in an earlier unit, "Congruence of Triangles and Quadrilaterals," in fifth grade. In this unit, we will use the hexagon-shaped toys students made for second graders to introduce the concept and properties of regular polygons and to develop strategies for drawing those shapes.

For circles, through investigation of concrete examples and through drawing circles and measuring the circumference, students will notice that the circumference is approximately 3.14 times the diameter and will summarize the relationship between circumference and diameter in a concrete formula.

Also, we thought students would expand their understanding of circles through the issues that arise as they find the circumferences of many shapes, draw shapes, and find the connection between the circumference and the diameter.

Students will discover they can find the area of a circle from the radius and circumference in an activity that uses a diagram of a partitioned circle and draws on an area formula and the relationship between circumference and diameter students have previously learned.

In addition, we want to provide a place where students can develop their own questions as they find the area of many large shapes, can notice the relationship between radius and area, and can make shapes themselves and find their areas.

We will use team-teaching to support these activities.

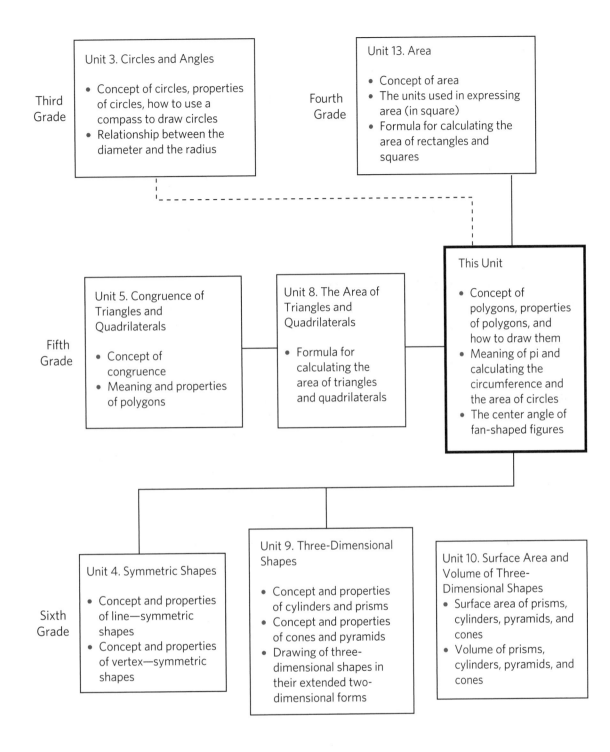

Third Grade

Unit 3. Circles and Angles

- Concept of circles, properties of circles, how to use a compass to draw circles
- Relationship between the diameter and the radius

Fourth Grade

Unit 13. Area

- Concept of area
- The units used in expressing area (in square)
- Formula for calculating the area of rectangles and squares

This Unit

- Concept of polygons, properties of polygons, and how to draw them
- Meaning of pi and calculating the circumference and the area of circles
- The center angle of fan-shaped figures

Fifth Grade

Unit 5. Congruence of Triangles and Quadrilaterals

- Concept of congruence
- Meaning and properties of polygons

Unit 8. The Area of Triangles and Quadrilaterals

- Formula for calculating the area of triangles and quadrilaterals

Sixth Grade

Unit 4. Symmetric Shapes

- Concept and properties of line—symmetric shapes
- Concept and properties of vertex—symmetric shapes

Unit 9. Three-Dimensional Shapes

- Concept and properties of cylinders and prisms
- Concept and properties of cones and pyramids
- Drawing of three-dimensional shapes in their extended two-dimensional forms

Unit 10. Surface Area and Volume of Three-Dimensional Shapes

- Surface area of prisms, cylinders, pyramids, and cones
- Volume of prisms, cylinders, pyramids, and cones

3. Goals of the Unit

Interest, desire to learn, and attitude. Students will actively grapple with the task of drawing regular polygons and will take the initiative to find the areas and circumferences of polygons of different sizes and shapes.

Mathematical thinking. Students will devise ways to draw regular polygons using a circle and will be able to consider the relationship of a circle's circumference and area to its diameter/radius.

Expression and performance. Students will draw regular polygons using a circle and be able to find the circumference and area of circles.

Knowledge and understanding. Students will understand how to draw regular polygons using a circle; also, students will understand circumference, the relationship between circumference and diameter, the meaning of pi, and the formula for calculating the area of a circle.

4. Current Situation of the Students

Although the fifth-grade students were reassigned to new homerooms, it is the third straight year this homeroom teacher has been assigned to their grade. The children in this class are cheerful and gentle, work hard to grasp various things, and are willing to learn different things. Because there are individual differences in their expression of thoughts, we are eager for students to have opportunities to express themselves.

Concerning the attitude of the students toward math, results from a survey showed that 73.5 percent of the class said they "like it very much" or "like it" and 26.5 percent said they "tend to dislike it" or "dislike it." That is, about one-fourth of the children have some kind of resistance toward math. In addition, many children in the class indicated dislike of "using what we've learned to solve new problems" and "deriving rules and formulas from a variety of problems." However, in the Division of Decimals unit, the students enjoyed problem solving as they discovered a principle, and many students actively applied prior learning to figure out the area of new shapes in the Area of Triangles and Quadrangles unit. There were also more students actively trying to figure out the areas of the drawings. We hope that the students will try to think for themselves and will experience the joy of finding new things through interacting with their peers.

We also hope that students will value having their own ideas and feel pleasure in discovering new things while working with friends.

5. Unit Plan (Twelve Hours of Lessons)

HOUR	OBJECTIVE	MAIN ACTIVITY	NATURE OF INSTRUCTION
1 to 3	To understand the concept and characteristics of polygons To understand how to construct polygons from circles and to actually construct polygons from circles	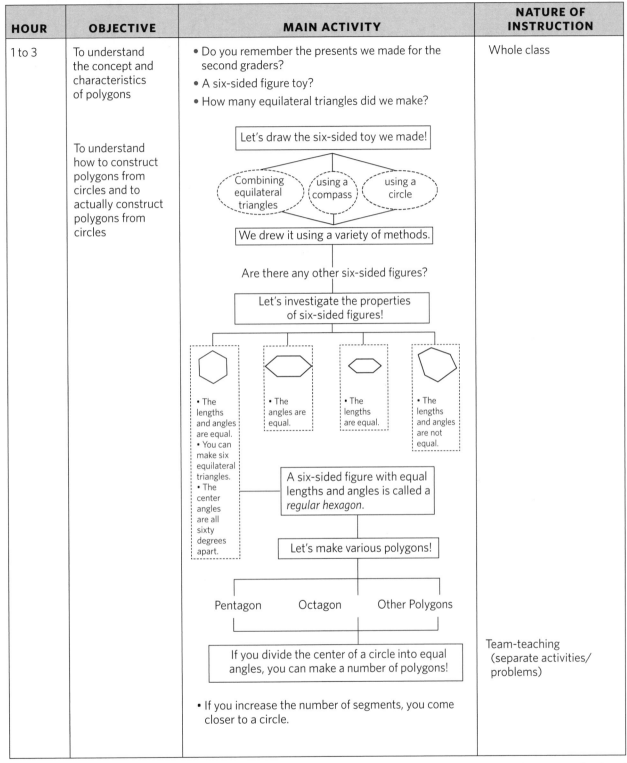	Whole class Team-teaching (separate activities/ problems)

(continues)

HOUR	OBJECTIVE	MAIN ACTIVITY	NATURE OF INSTRUCTION
4 to 5	To understand the meaning of circumference and π	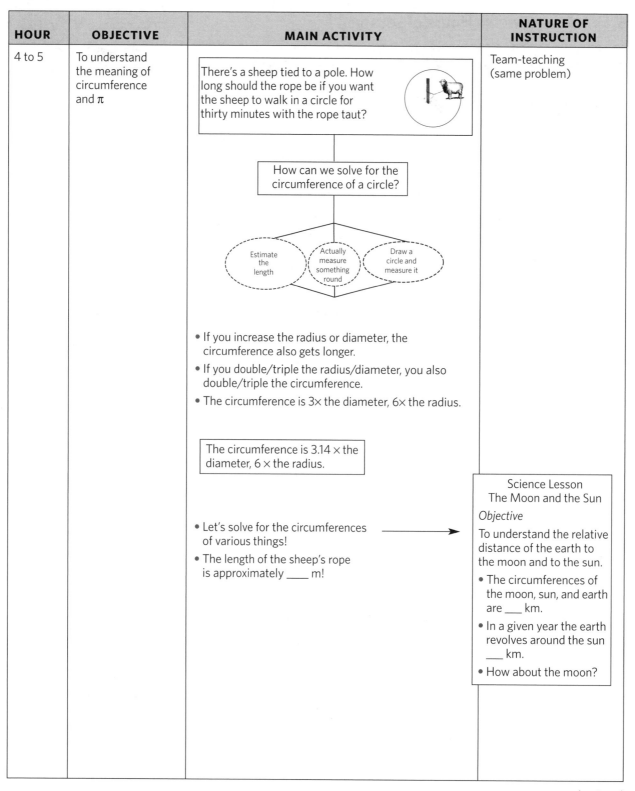	Team-teaching (same problem)

There's a sheep tied to a pole. How long should the rope be if you want the sheep to walk in a circle for thirty minutes with the rope taut?

How can we solve for the circumference of a circle?

Estimate the length

Actually measure something round

Draw a circle and measure it

• If you increase the radius or diameter, the circumference also gets longer.
• If you double/triple the radius/diameter, you also double/triple the circumference.
• The circumference is 3× the diameter, 6× the radius.

The circumference is 3.14 × the diameter, 6 × the radius.

• Let's solve for the circumferences of various things!
• The length of the sheep's rope is approximately ____ m!

Science Lesson
The Moon and the Sun
Objective
To understand the relative distance of the earth to the moon and to the sun.
• The circumferences of the moon, sun, and earth are ___ km.
• In a given year the earth revolves around the sun ___ km.
• How about the moon?

(continues)

APPENDIX K – MATHEMATICS TEACHING-LEARNING PLAN

HOUR	OBJECTIVE	MAIN ACTIVITY	NATURE OF INSTRUCTION
6 to 7	To solve the lengths of various circles To develop students' understanding of the relationship between diameter and circumference (Today's lesson)	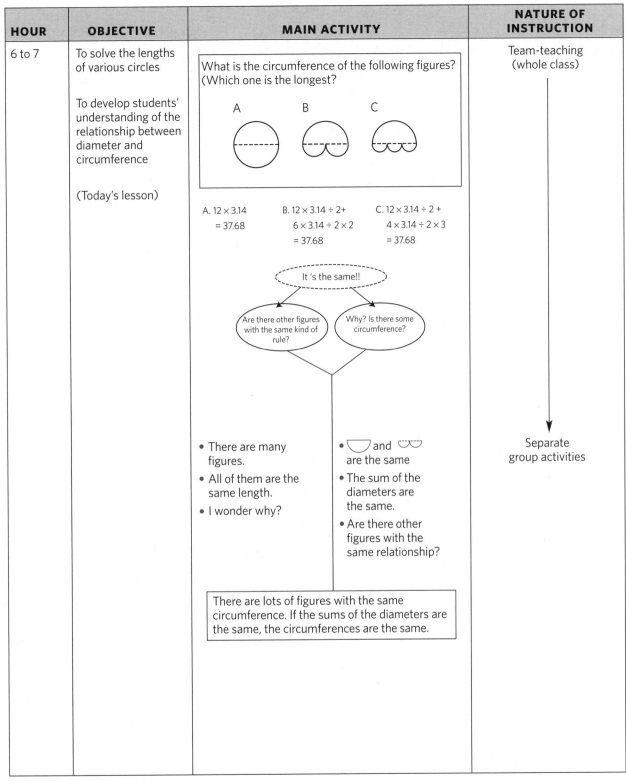	Team-teaching (whole class) ↓ Separate group activities

(continues)

HOUR	OBJECTIVE	MAIN ACTIVITY	NATURE OF INSTRUCTION
8 to 9	To understand how to solve for the area of a circle using estimation and transformation	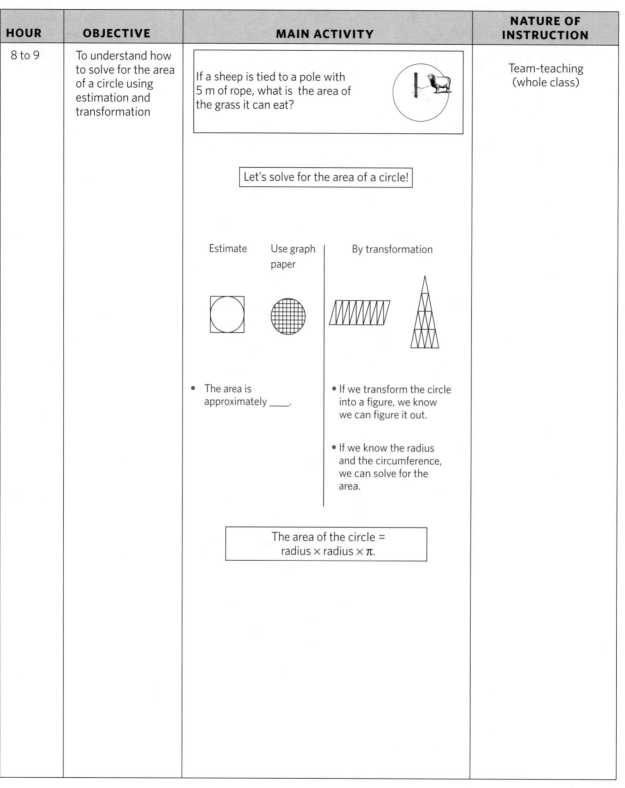	Team-teaching (whole class)

HOUR	OBJECTIVE	MAIN ACTIVITY	NATURE OF INSTRUCTION
10 to 12	To determine the area of a number of figures involving circles To develop students' understanding of the relationship between radius and the area of the circle	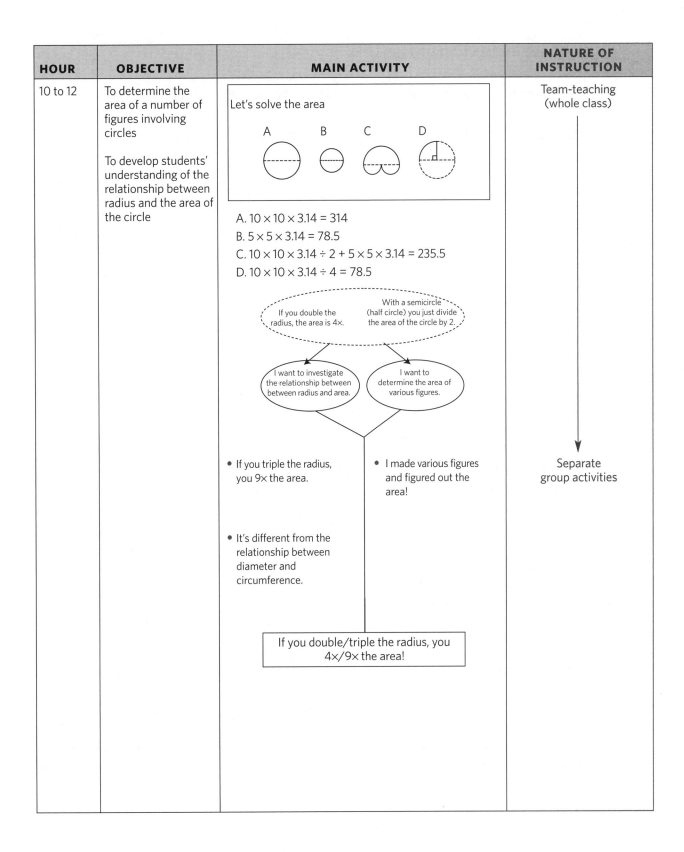	Team-teaching (whole class) Separate group activities

6. About Instruction of This Unit

Viewpoint 1: Develop learning activities suitable to diverse problem-solving approaches.

Teaching Materials That Give Birth to "Problem Finding"

In the beginning of November, the fifth graders made simple toys out of paper and presented them as gifts to second graders. By recalling those hexagonal toys at the introduction of the unit, we turned students' attention to the characteristics of regular polygons and ways to draw them.

After students learned how to find circumference, they were shown three different shapes that, in contrast to their expectations, had identical circumferences. From that surprise, individual students developed a problem consciousness and became able to notice issues like "How could it be that the shapes were different yet the circumferences the same?" and "Are there other shapes that have the same circumference?"

During the study of the area of circles, four figures were provided. After students found the areas, the unit was designed to enable them to actively pursue important issues they noticed, as they made a variety of figures and calculated their areas and as they grasped the relation between radius and area by comparing it with the relation between circumference and diameter.

Through these learning approaches, we believed that children would expand their understanding of circles, find circles interesting, and also build their own capacity for continued, self-initiated learning. Also, by presenting the shapes they discovered to the class, we expected students to deepen their motivation and reflect on their learning.

Unit Structure That Promotes a Climate of Mutual Improvement

For students to continue to learn, a unit structure is needed in which students keep improving their ideas as they seek better solution methods and generalizations. For this, solitary learning is not sufficient, and we wanted this unit to enable students to relate their ideas to one another and recognize and build on the strengths of each other's ideas, in turn increasing the overall strength of the class.

In this unit, after discovering the methods for finding circumference and area of the circle, students formulate their own questions and think about new shapes using circles or build on what they have previously learned. They then can test out their ideas through interaction with peers and find new ideas.

We want students to be able to experience the sense of satisfaction and joy that comes from discovering something new, in an environment where problems are born from students' authentic experiences. We want students to taste the pleasure of thinking together in an environment where they can make their own ideas more accurate and can find better ideas and improve them with classmates. To create that kind of setting, it is important that each individual child has his or her own ideas. Students understand their own strengths and those of classmates for the first time when they bring their own ideas to discussion, so we emphasized sufficient time to think individually before interaction.

We designated points when it would be good for students to discuss their work in small groups, so that this work would connect to the larger discussion of the class—for example: Did you discover anything? Is there anything that is always true (generalizing)?

During whole-class discussion, teachers should endeavor to enliven the discussion by observing students' activities and giving appropriate support (e.g., by commending previously learned knowledge; by aiding connections when students are generalizing, comparing, or deliberating; and by supporting discoveries).

We also strategized ways to create an environment in which students could always exchange ideas easily. For example, blackboard magnets (with student names) enabled students to see each other's ideas and the discussion issues, and a table workspace was created.

Team-Teaching That Responds to Student Diversity

Each individual child has different ideas when he or she approaches a problem. Especially in mathematics, there are large individual differences in depth and speed of understanding of the topic. Although we want to respond to students' individual differences in style and speed of learning, and also to honor the individual differences in their ideas, at the same time, we want to enable all students to experience firsthand the pleasure of reasoning. For this, we believe it is effective to have a team of two teachers work together. For this reason, we chose team-teaching for this unit (with different forms of team-teaching, such as joint activity and separate roles by task or issue). This lesson uses team-teaching (separate roles, divided by issue) in the section of the lesson designed to expand students' viewpoints and thinking about circles.

To support students in this way and respond to each individual child, the teachers' roles have been defined in advance, and the strategies for observation and support of students agreed upon. Teachers will confer as needed during class to give the best support to students.

> Viewpoint 2: The evaluation and support by teachers enables individual students to enjoy learning and improvement.

Valuing Each Child's Particular Characteristics

Each student has special qualities. To preserve these and at the same time expand the student's potential, it is necessary to have a viewpoint from which to see that student. To accomplish this, using the class list we chose as a focus of observation each student's approach to learning, interest and desire to learn, and expressive capacity.

In addition, because more than one teacher is involved, the viewpoint for evaluation and method of guidance were agreed on before teaching, so that we can respond softly to each student. To verify and promote mathematical thinking, it is particularly important for the instructor to facilitate connections with previous learning and among viewpoints in debates/comparisons. In addition, for learning to advance, it is important for students to want to learn from each other and to notice their own and each other's strengths.

Self-Evaluation Strategies That Enable Students to Experience Their Strengths

We tried to devise self-evaluations that would enable students to reflect on their learning and themselves. We want students to both taste their own strengths and feel a sense of "I can do it if I try," but also have a desire to go further. We want them to reflect not just on themselves, but on the strengths of their classmates during discussion, and to develop a spirit of recognizing each other and nurturing one another's growth.

With respect to evaluation, we want students to assess themselves both from the viewpoint we establish and also to choose their own viewpoint for reflection on their learning and write in a journal.

Self-Evaluation Card

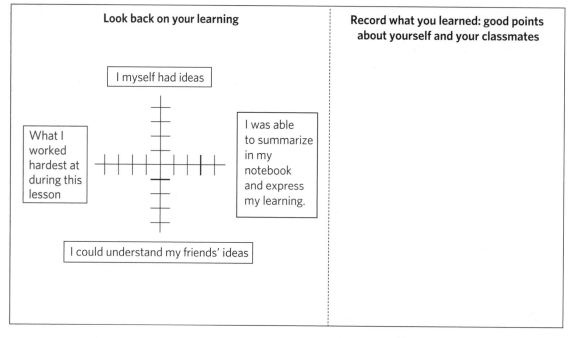

7. Lesson Goals for Today's Lesson (Seventh of Twelve Lessons in Unit)

1. While finding the circumferences of various figures made of circles, to notice the relationship between diameter and circumference and to try to find more shapes with equal circumferences.

2. To try expand one's own thinking by learning with classmates.

8. Lesson Plan for Today's Lesson

LESSON FLOW	ROLE OF TEACHER(S)

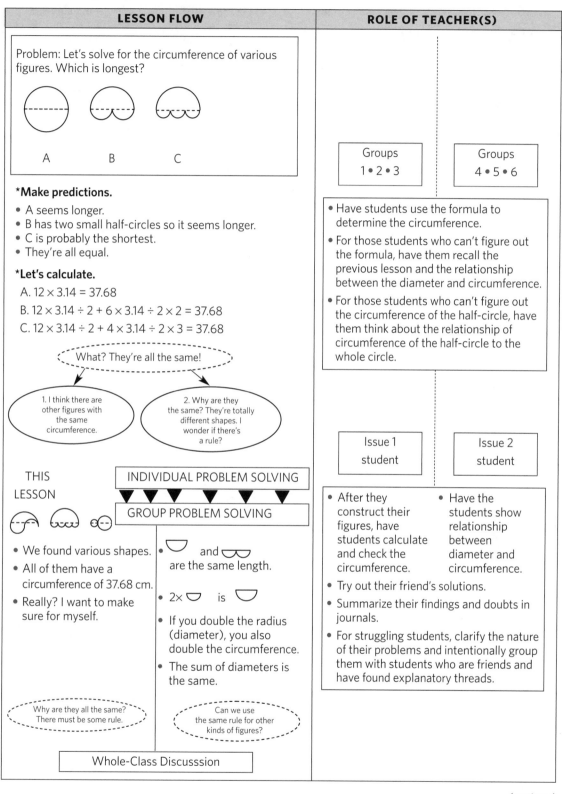

LESSON FLOW

Problem: Let's solve for the circumference of various figures. Which is longest?

A   B   C

*Make predictions.

- A seems longer.
- B has two small half-circles so it seems longer.
- C is probably the shortest.
- They're all equal.

*Let's calculate.

A. $12 \times 3.14 = 37.68$

B. $12 \times 3.14 \div 2 + 6 \times 3.14 \div 2 \times 2 = 37.68$

C. $12 \times 3.14 \div 2 + 4 \times 3.14 \div 2 \times 3 = 37.68$

What? They're all the same!

1. I think there are other figures with the same circumference.

2. Why are they the same? They're totally different shapes. I wonder if there's a rule?

THIS LESSON

INDIVIDUAL PROBLEM SOLVING

▼ ▼ ▼ ▼ ▼ ▼

GROUP PROBLEM SOLVING

- We found various shapes.
- All of them have a circumference of 37.68 cm.
- Really? I want to make sure for myself.

- ⌣ and ⌣ are the same length.

- $2 \times$ ⌣ is ⌣

- If you double the radius (diameter), you also double the circumference.

- The sum of diameters is the same.

Why are they all the same? There must be some rule.

Can we use the same rule for other kinds of figures?

Whole-Class Discusssion

ROLE OF TEACHER(S)

| Groups 1 • 2 • 3 | Groups 4 • 5 • 6 |

- Have students use the formula to determine the circumference.
- For those students who can't figure out the formula, have them recall the previous lesson and the relationship between the diameter and circumference.
- For those students who can't figure out the circumference of the half-circle, have them think about the relationship of circumference of the half-circle to the whole circle.

| Issue 1 student | Issue 2 student |

- After they construct their figures, have students calculate and check the circumference.
- Have the students show relationship between diameter and circumference.
- Try out their friend's solutions.
- Summarize their findings and doubts in journals.
- For struggling students, clarify the nature of their problems and intentionally group them with students who are friends and have found explanatory threads.

(continues)

LESSON FLOW	**ROLE OF TEACHER(S)**	
* Discuss what they found in their small groups. • We discovered a number of shapes with the same circumference. • If you double or triple the radius (diameter), you also double or triple the circumference. > We found various shapes with same circumference. If the sum of the diameters is the same, the circumference is the same. *** Reflection/summary.**	• Have students present their findings, write them on the blackboard.	• Assess students. • Help prepare students for their presentation.
	Depending on the situation and students, simultaneously: • Help students realize their own and friends' effort. • Motivate students for next lesson.	

APPENDIX K – MATHEMATICS TEACHING-LEARNING PLAN

Teaching-Learning Plan Template

Team Members:

Instructor:
Date:
Grade Level:

1. Title of Lesson:

2. Research Theme* (Long-term Goals), Broad Subject Matter Goals, Lesson Goals:
   (*Appendix J provides information on research theme development.)

3. Lesson Rationale: Why we chose to focus on this topic and goals. (For example, what is difficult about learning/teaching this topic? What do we notice about students currently as learners?) Why we designed the lesson as shown below.

4. How does students' understanding of this topic develop? For example, how does this lesson fit within a unit? How does it fit within students' experiences in prior and subsequent grades?

5. Relationship of the Lesson to State (or Other) Standards

6. Lesson Design:

STUDENT LEARNING ACTIVITIES	ANTICIPATED STUDENT REPONSES AND TEACHER RESPONSE	POINTS TO NOTICE (EVALUATION)

7. Data collection points during the lesson observation.

- Our team will collect data on:

- Outside observers are asked to collect data on:

Conclusion: What we have learned from this lesson study process:

Research Map Template

Map of Research Conception

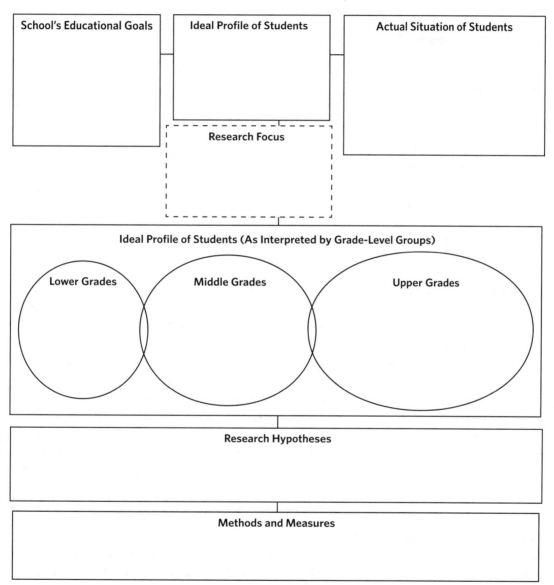

School's Educational Goals

Ideal Profile of Students

Actual Situation of Students

Research Focus

Ideal Profile of Students (As Interpreted by Grade-Level Groups)

Lower Grades

Middle Grades

Upper Grades

Research Hypotheses

Methods and Measures

Science Teaching-Learning Plan

Featured on the Videotape "Can You Lift 100 Kilograms?"(Grade 5)*

1. Unit: The Way Levers Work

2. Unit Objectives

Enable students to investigate the design and operation of levers by changing the position from which effort is exerted and the amount of effort. To learn that:

A. If you change the position of the weight, the angle of the lever changes, even though the heaviness of the weight remains the same.

B. The lever has three major points: the fulcrum, the point of effort, and the point of resistance.

C. In the operation of a lever, there is a relationship between the amount of effort exerted and position from which effort it is exerted. When the lever balances, the amount and position of effort are related to each other according to a constant principle.

3. Connection with Research Focus

In their daily lives, the children use tools that involve the lever principle without realizing it. Their use of these tools is thus based upon their experience. We believe that in this unit of study, by discovering the rules and laws of the lever, the children will be able to experience anew the usefulness of tools that employ the lever principle.

If the children can discover that the rules and laws of nature are at work even in the commonplace tools of everyday life, it should be a joyful experience for them.

Also, the children will be divided into groups of several children each, and there will be a number of objectives that can only be achieved through cooperating and working together. In the midst of that activity, using the ideas of their classmates for reference, we think that the students will come to be able to give expression to ideas deeper than their own (initial) thoughts, and that is why we decided upon this unit.

4. Actual Situation of the Students

There are a lot of children who look forward to science classes because there are so many experiments and so much hands-on work involved. The boys and girls generally get along well

---

*Available at www.lessonresearch.net.

---

and work together cooperatively, but there are one or two children in the class who have difficulty entering smoothly into such groups.

Generally, the students are serious and willing to work hard at whatever they are directed to do, but they also tend to lack the desire to come up with and try out their own ideas independently. It is noticeable that some students cannot make presentations confidently, because they don't have their own firm ideas and predictions.

5. Steps to Accomplish Our (Research) Focus

(1) Strategies for the Learning Process

Based on the actual situation of the students, our plan of instruction aims to have students grapple naturally with the subject.

Our overall plan is to enter the unit from learning that interests and fascinates the children, then pursue the scientific facts, and then end with learning that is useful in their everyday lives. We hope to maintain the students' interest through this unit design.

Part One of the Unit (Lessons 1–4)

In part one of the unit, we planned the following learning flow:

Grasp the problem → Make a prediction → Discuss → Verify → Consolidate → Grasp new issue

Through this "learning flow" children should be able to grasp the problem at hand as their own problem, and take the initiative in solving it.

Part Two of the Unit (Lessons 5–7)

In part two, by using (calibrated) laboratory levers, allow the children to discover the rules by which the lever slants and balances.

Part Three of the Unit (Lessons 8–9)

In part three, we plan to help the children realize that there are a great many tools that employ the lever principle even in their ordinary environments, so that in their everyday lives they could put into practice what they learn. In the new National Course of Study, the "weight and balance" unit presently studied at the fourth grade will be combined into this unit. With that in mind, we included the balance scale in this unit.

(2) Strategies for Curriculum Materials

Because we are trying to use materials from their everyday environment to get them interested, we have chosen to use sandbags for the weights. The students already have the experience of trying to move sandbags during their physical education classes. In addition, moving the heavy sandbags is a task that will give the students a very clear sense of the problem at hand. Furthermore, using a pole in order to move these sandbags will make the students more aware that the objects around them can, with a little engineering, become useful tools.

Among the tools that employ the lever principle, we choose one (the can-crusher) that relates to the new "environmentally aware" recycling lifestyle of modern children.

(3) Strategies for Support and Evaluation

We will prepare a worksheet for each problem in the lesson and observe the depth and flow of the students' thoughts. Since the students who do not have the confidence to come up with and share their own ideas will be writing them down on the worksheet, they will be able to organize their own ideas and they will leave written evidence regarding the process via which their own thinking deepened through group discussion.

Also, we want to value the *tsubuyaki* (under-breath exclamations) of the children during the experiments. Since this unit is supported by team teaching, we hope that we can hear more of the students' *tsubuyaki* and, by transmitting them to the other students, help each of the individual students to deepen their own thoughts.

(4) Strategies for the Learning Activities

Depending on the content of a lesson, there are many different ways to group children. We decided that for this unit we want to group together children who came up with similar first ideas for solving the problem. This will make the discussions which take place within each group particularly important; by relating to other students who have similar ideas, the students should thus be able both to deepen and modify their own thoughts.

Also, feelings of competition among groups may lead students to aim at higher goals and work all the harder at devising their own group's experimental methods.

6. Plan of Instruction [UNIT PLAN]

LESSON	LEARNING ACTIVITY	METHODS; POINTS TO NOTICE
1.	**Part 1: Let's Try Moving Heavy Objects** *What should be done in order to lift a heavy object off the ground?* • How heavy is it? • Which tools should be used? • Which way should it be done?	(3) Worksheet (2) Sandbags
2. **(The Research Lesson)** 3.	*Let's really try moving it.* • Will it lift? • How does it feel? • Isn't there an easier way to lift it? • Let's try the pole. • Let's try changing the position we lift from. • Let's change the place it's supported. • Let's see how the weight feels.	(4) Groups of children with the same ideas (2) Sandbags, poles, and other equipment based on the children's ideas (3) Worksheet: Children's Utterances
4.	*Let's find the rules for moving heaving objects.* • Let's think about the relation between the • Fulcrum and the point of effort. • Let's think about the power put into the point of effort.	
5.	**Part 2: What Kind of Rules Govern the Balance of the Lever?** *Let's discover the rules of the lever when it is tilted.* • Let's think about which way it tilts when we change the distance between the fulcrum and the point of resistance and fulcrum and point of effort, and when we vary the weight of the object to be lifted.	(3) Worksheet: Children's Utterances
6.	*Let's discover the rules of the lever when it is balanced.* • Let's try to balance the lever by changing the distance between fulcrum and point of resistance and between fulcrum and point of effort, and by varying the weight of the object to be lifted.	(3) Worksheet: Children's Utterances

(continues)

LESSON	LEARNING ACTIVITY	METHODS; POINTS TO NOTICE
7.	*Let's put together the rules of the lever when balanced and when tilted.* • Let's put together our understanding: the lever tilts or balances according to the value on the left and right arms on: "Weight of the Object" x "Distance from the Fulcrum"	
	Part Three: Let's Search for Tools That Use the Lever Principle	
8.	*Let's try using some tools that employ the principle of the lever when it is balanced.* • Let's try using a balance scale.	(1) Strategies for the Learning Process: The Balance Scale
9.	*Let's try using some tools that employ the principle of the lever when it is tilted.* • Let's try a can-crusher. • Let's try a bottle-cap remover. • Let's try prying nails. • Let's try pliers. • Let's try scissors. • Let's try tweezers.	(2) Strategies for Curriculum Materials: The Can-Crusher
	(1) Strategies for Learning Process (2) Strategies for Curriculum Materials (3) Strategies for Support and Evaluation (4) Strategies for Student Activities	

APPENDIX N – SCIENCE TEACHING-LEARNING PLAN

7. Today's Lesson

1) The Aims of this Lesson

1. For students to actively consider how to use objects easily after finding that it's really hard to lift a heavy object by hand.

2. For students to deepen their own thinking by expressing their ideas to others.

3. For students to pay attention to safety and to cooperate with their friends while conducting experiments.

2) The Development of this Lesson

TEACHER 1 ACTIVITY	LEARNING ACTIVITY	MEANS AND POINTS TO NOTICE	TEACHER 2 ACTIVITY
Overall Guidance: Check the conditions of the experiment

Give guidance and help to each of the groups

Overall Guidance: Direct their progress toward the next experiment.

Give guidance and support to groups working on "Floor Sandbag #1" | *Try lifting the "Floor Sandbag #1":*
• Using tools from their everyday environments
• Having just one person lift it
• By taking turns, making sure that every group member can lift it

Make sure to see that it has really been lifted.
• The group that lifted it tries "Floor Sandbag #2."
• If they could not lift it, they try finding an easier way to lift "Floor Sandbag #1," and then take the challenge again.

Discover that a pole can be put to good use in order to move heavy objects. | ("Sandbag #1" weighs about 30 kg.)

The groups, based on the ideas they came up with earlier, carry out their experiments.

Take turns to fill out their results on the worksheets, referring to each other's ideas. ("Floor Sandbag #2 weighs about 100 kg.")

Take turns to fill out their results on the worksheets, referring to each other's ideas. | Give guidance and help to each of the groups.

Give guidance and support to groups working on "Floor Sandbag #2."

Overall Guidance: Point out the groups that have used the pole and lifted the weight. |

3) Evaluation of this Lesson

1. After finding that it's very hard to lift a heavy object by hand, did the students actively consider how to use the pole to lift heavy objects easily?

2. Were the students able to deepen their thinking process by talking about their ideas with friends?

3. Were the students able to cooperate and attend to safety while performing the experiments?

8. Student Groups for Experiments

The original lesson plan provides the names of all students in each group. It also provides eight examples of student plans for lifting the sandbag.

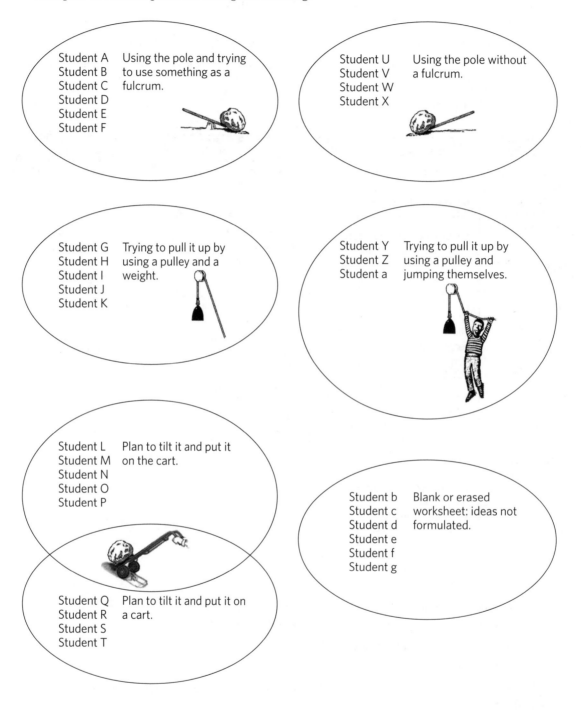

Student A
Student B
Student C
Student D
Student E
Student F

Using the pole and trying to use something as a fulcrum.

Student U
Student V
Student W
Student X

Using the pole without a fulcrum.

Student G
Student H
Student I
Student J
Student K

Trying to pull it up by using a pulley and a weight.

Student Y
Student Z
Student a

Trying to pull it up by using a pulley and jumping themselves.

Student L
Student M
Student N
Student O
Student P

Plan to tilt it and put it on the cart.

Student b
Student c
Student d
Student e
Student f
Student g

Blank or erased worksheet: ideas not formulated.

Student Q
Student R
Student S
Student T

Plan to tilt it and put it on a cart.

About Team-Teaching

Starting this year, eight hours of team teaching instruction per week has been introduced into our school. This year the fifth- and sixth-grade science classes were suited to the team teaching schedule, and we commenced this program in April. After considering the schedule and content, we scheduled team teaching out as follows:

1st & 3rd Semesters ...... Sixth grade   3 hours per week X 2 classes

2nd Semester.................. Fifth grade   3 hours per week X 2 classes

The remaining two hours are for class preparation.

When we actually carried out team teaching, we noticed several things we hadn't realized previously about team teaching. They are outlined as follows:

STRONG POINTS	WEAK POINTS
• There are more opportunities to try out new kinds of experiments. • We had three perspectives on science learning at our grade level, and we could divide the preparations among us. • The safety of the lessons was increased. • It was easier to hear the students' utterances, and so easier to give them support.	• Depending on the content of the lessons, such as continuing observation, or things related to weather and temperature, it is sometimes easier for the class teacher to conduct the lesson. • Figuring out how to divide the time is difficult. • Making the schedule for the use of the science classroom was also difficult. • There is no time for planning.

Anticipating Student Responses

Learning to anticipate, observe, and analyze student thinking is a central part of lesson study. As teachers learn to view an activity from a student's perspective and trace the student's process of knowledge development, many insights into the effectiveness of instructional strategies and tools become possible. Learning to see a lesson from the perspective of the students (not just the teacher moves and the curriculum goals) is a paradigm shift for many teachers. We have often heard teachers comment during the postlesson discussion of the research lesson, "If only we had anticipated the student responses, or done the activity ourselves, we would have seen that problem coming."

Teachers new to lesson study often rush through or skip doing the activity students will do during the lesson. This is not surprising since we seldom have the luxury of trying out an activity ourselves to consider it from the perspective of students. However, many important insights can be gained from this practice that will enable us to design a more effective lesson.

To anticipate student responses, we suggest the following steps:

1. Each member of the planning team should independently do the activity intended for the research lesson.

2. Give each member an opportunity to share how they approached the activity, and what they experienced. Usually in a group of four to six teachers, there will be a variety of strategies. Teachers' responses will begin to shed light on how different students may approach the activity.

3. Imagine different students you know and discuss how they might experience the activity. What successes and difficulties will students encounter? What is a successful process and outcome for this task? How will you measure success?

4. The point of anticipating student responses is *not* to design the activity so that students won't struggle or so that misconceptions won't emerge, but rather to give teachers an opportunity to plan how they will respond and to think about what kind of struggles and misconception may be key to students' learning during the lesson. Eliciting struggles and misconceptions can be an intentional element of the lesson. Discuss the instructional strategies and options that might facilitate the student learning as struggles and misconceptions emerge.

5. If you adjust the lesson activity based on this exercise, try the lesson activity again to check again for anticipated student responses.

6. Record the anticipated student responses and teacher responses in the lesson plan. Document these adjustments in your lesson rationale.

Data Collection Guide

The following questions will help you identify the data to be collected by observers during the lesson.

1. What data will help you understand your students' progress on your lesson goals, broad subject matter goals, and long-term goals (research theme)?

2. Would a prepared data collection form facilitate observation? (For example, a form that lists strategies you anticipate or a seating chart to record conversation pathways.)

3. What student work will be collected at the end of the lesson? (For example, an exit slip with a targeted question a student journal, or a piece of writing.)

4. How will material presented on the blackboard or in other venues be captured (for example, by observers, or by using and retaining chart paper)?

5. What are the individual assignments of the lesson study team? Will one person transcribe the lesson and keep a timeline of lesson events? Will observers be assigned to observe specific students or groups?

Lesson Observation Log

Title of lesson:

Goals of the lesson:

Observation objectives:

TIME	OBSERVATION	SIGNIFICANCE

TIME	OBSERVATION	SIGNIFICANCE

Conclusions:

Further questions raised:

References

Ball, D. L. 1996. "Teacher Learning and the Mathematics Reforms: What We Think We Know and What We Need to Learn." *Phi Delta Kappan* (March): 505.

Brill, S., and A. McCartney. 2008. "Stopping the Revolving Door: Increasing Teacher Retention." *Politics and Policy* 36: 750–774.

Coeyman, M. 2000. "US School, Japanese Methods." *Christian Science Monitor* (May 23).

Cohen, D. K., and D. L. Ball. 2000, April. Instructional Innovation: Reconsidering the Story. Paper presented at the meeting of the American Educational Research Association, New Orleans.

Cossey, R., and P. Tucher. 2005. "Teaching to Collaborate, Collaborating to Teach." In L. R. Kroll, R. Cossey, D. M. Donahue, T. Galguera, V. K. LaBoskey, A. E. Richert, and P. Tucher (Eds.), *Teaching as Principals Practice: Managing Complexity for Social Justice*, 105–120. Thousand Oaks, CA: Sage.

Council for Basic Education. 2000. "The Eye of the Storm: Improving Teaching Practices to Achieve Higher Standards." Briefing book, Wingspread Conference, September 24–27, Racine, WI.

Darling-Hammond, L. 1999. "Professional Development for Teachers: Setting the Stage for Learning from Teaching." Santa Cruz, CA: The Center for the Future of Teaching and Learning. Available at: www.cftl.org/documents/Darling_Hammond_paper.pdf.

Darling-Hammond, L., and M. W. McLaughlin. 1995. "Policies That Support Professional Development in an Era of Reform." *Phi Delta Kappan* 76 (8): 597–604.

Darling-Hammond, L., R. C. Wei, A. Andree, N. Richardson, and S. Orphanos. 2009. *Professional Learning in the Learning Profession: A Status Report on Teacher Development in the United States and Abroad.* Report published by the National Staff Development Council (NSDC) and The School Redesign Network at Stanford University.

Development Studies Center. 1994. *At Home in Our Schools: A Guide to Schoolwide Activities That Build Community.* Oakland, CA: Development Studies Center.

Driscoll, M., R. W. DiMatteo, J. Nikula, M. Egan, J. Mark, and G. Kelemanik. 2007. *The Fostering Geometric Thinking Toolkit.* Portsmouth, NH: Heinemann.

Dubin, J. 2009. "American Teachers Embrace the Japanese Art of Lesson Study." *American Educator* (Fall): 30–34.

Elmore, R. 1999–2000. "Building a New Structure for School Leadership." *American Educator* 23 (4): 12.

Fernandez, C., J. Cannon, and S. Chokshi. 2003. "A U.S.-Japan Lesson Study Collaborative Reaveals Critical Lenses for Examining Practice." *Teaching and Teacher Education* (19): 171–185.

Fernandez, C., S. Chokshi, J. Cannon, and M. Yoshida. 2001. "Learning About Lesson Study in the United States." In *New and Old Voices on Japanese Education*, edited by E. Beauchamp. Armonk, NY: M. E. Sharpe.

Fernandez, C., and M. Yoshida. 2004. *Lesson Study: A Japanese Approach to Improving Mathematics Teaching and Learning.* Mahwah, NJ: Lawrence Erlbaum.

Foster, D., and A. Poppers. 2009. *Using Formative Assessment to Drive Learning. The Silicon Valley Mathematics Initiative: A Twelve-Year Research and Development Project.* Palo Alto, CA: The Noyce Foundation.

Franke, M., T. Carpenter, E. Fennema, E. Ansell, and J. Behrend. 1998. "Understanding Teachers' Self-Sustaining Generative, Change in the Context of Professional Development." *Teaching and Teacher Education* 14 (1): 67–80.

Germain-McCarthy, Y. 2001. *Bringing the NCTM Standards to Life: Exemplary Practices for Middle Schools*. Larchmont, NY: Eye on Education.

Gewertz, C. 2010. "Aligning Standards and Curriculum Begets Questions." *Education Week, 29* 32 (May 19): 122.

Gorman, J., J. Mark, and J. Nikula. 2010. *Lesson Study in Practice: A Mathematics Staff Development Course*. Portsmouth, NH: Heinemann.

Hiebert, J., R. Gallimore, and J. W. Stigler. 2002. "A Knowledge Base for the Teaching Profession: What Would It Look Like and How Can We Get One?" *Educational Researcher* 31 (5): 3–15.

Hironaka, H., and Y. Sugiyama. 2006. *Mathematics for Elementary School, Grades 1–6*. Tokyo: Tokyo Shoseki Co. Ltd. (English language version available at www.global edresources.com).

Hurd, J., and L. Ricciardo-Musso. 2005. "Teacher-Led Professional Development in Literacy Instruction." *Language Arts* 82 (5): 388–95.

Ishikawa, K., K. Hayakawa, T. Fujinaka, T. Nakamura, I. Moriya, and A. Takii. 2001. "Nihon suagaku kyouiku gakkai zasshi [Considering the nature of lesson study in elementary schools]." *Journal of Japan Society of Mathematical Education* 84 (4): 14–23 (in Japanese).

Lewis, C. 1995. *Educating Hearts and Minds: Reflections on Japanese Preschool and Elementary Education*. New York: Cambridge University Press.

Lewis, C., K. Akita, and M. Sato. 2010. "Lesson Study as a Human Science." In W. Penuel and K. O'Connor (Eds.) Learning Research as a Human Science. *National Society for the Study of Education Yearbook* 109 (1): 222–37. http://nsse-chicago.org.

Lewis, C., and R. Perry. 2009/2010. "Building a Knowledge Base for Teaching: Design and Test of Research-Based Toolkits to Support Lesson Study." Paper presented at the annual meeting of the American Educational Research Association. April 2009, June 2010.

Lewis, C., R. Perry, S. Friedkin, L. Fisher, J. Disston, and D. Foster. 2012. "Building Knowledge and Professional Community Through Lesson Study." In J. M. Bay-Williams (Ed.), *2012 NCTM Yearbook*. Reston, VA: National Council of Teachers of Mathematics.

Lewis, C., R. Perry, and J. Hurd. 2009. "Improving Mathematics Instruction Through Lesson Study: A Theoretical Model and North American Case." *Journal of Mathematics Teacher Education* 12 (4): 285–304.

Lewis, C., R. Perry, J. Hurd, and M. P. O'Connell. 2006. "Lesson Study Comes of Age in North America." *Phi Delta Kappan* (December): 273–81.

Lewis, C., E. Schaps, and M. Watson. 1995. "Beyond the Pendulum: Creating Caring and Challenging Schools." *Phi Delta Kappan* 76: 547–54.

———. 1999. "Recapturing Education's Full Mission: Educating for Social, Ethical, and Intellectual Development." In *Instructional-Design Theories and Models: A New Paradigm of Instructional Theory*, edited by C. Reigeluth, 511–39. Mahwah, NJ: Lawrence Erlbaum.

Lewis, C., and I. Tsuchida. 1997. "Planned Educational Change in Japan: The Shift to Student-Centered Elementary Science." *Journal of Educational Policy* 12 (5): 313–31.

Liptak, L. 2005. "For Principals: Critical Elements." In P. Wang-Iverson and M. Yoshida (Eds.), *Building Our Understanding of Lesson Study*, 39–44.

Lo, M., P. Chik, and W. Pong. 2005. *For Each and Everyone: Catering for Individual Differences Through Learning Studies.* Hong Kong: Hong Kong University Press.

Ma, Liping. 2001. Remarks at Learn Globally, Teach Locally conference. Mid-Atlantic Eisenhower Consortium for Mathematics and Science Education at Research for Better Schools, Cherry Hill, NJ, April 23.

Machado, A. 2003. *There is No Road: Proverbs of Antonio Machado.* Translated by Mary Berg and Dennis Maloney. Buffalo, NY: White Pine Press. Retrieved January 3, 2011 from www.whitepine.org/noroad.pdf.

Mathematics Content Standards for California Public Schools Kindergarten Through Grade 12. Retrieved from http://www.cde.ca.gov/be/st/ss/documents/math standard.pdf.

Murata, A., 2010. Learning by Making Connections in Practice: A Case of Kindergarten Lesson Study. Paper under review.

Murata, A., and B. E. Pothen. (forthcoming). *Lesson Study Research and Practice: Learning Together.* Norwell, MA: Springer.

Nakamura, T. "Zadankai: Shougakkou ni okeru juugyou kenkyuu no arikata wo kangaeru" (Panel Discussion: Considering the Nature of Lesson Study in Elementary Schools). *Nihon Sugaku Kyouiku Gakkai Zasshi* (Journal of Japan Society of Mathematical Education) 84 (4): 14–23.

National Research Council. 2001. *Adding It Up: Helping Children Learn Mathematics.* Washington, DC: National Academy Press.

Ogden, N., C. Perkins, and D. Donahue. 2008. "Not a Peculiar Institution: Challenging Students' Assumptions About Slavery in U.S. History." *History Teacher* 41 (4): 469–89.

Perry, R., and C. Lewis. 2008. "What is successful adaptation of lesson study in the U.S.?" *Journal of Educational Change* 10 (4): 365–91.

———. 2010. "Building Demand for Research Through Lesson Study." In M. K. Stein and C. Coburn (Eds.), *Research and Practice in Education: Building Alliances, Bridging the Divide.* Lanham, MD: Rowman and Littlefield.

Pesick, S. 2005. "Lesson Study and the Teaching of American History: Connecting Professional Development and Classroom Practice." *Social Studies Review.* http://findarticles.com/p/articles/mi_qa 4033/15_200504/ai_n14800120/.

Sato, M., and M. Sato. 2001. *Jugyou wo tsukuru* (Creating Instruction). Tokyo: Gyousei Publishing.

Saunders, W. M., C. N. Goldenberg, and R. Gallimore. 2009. "Increasing Achievement by Focusing Grade Level Teams on Improving Classroom Learning: A Prospective, Qualitative Study of Title 1 Schools." *American Educational Research Journal* 4 (46): 1006–1033.

SCOE (Sonoma County Office of Education). 2009. *SCOE Bulletin.* Student interviews. Retrieved September 21, 2010 from http://www.scoe.org/files/bulletin-1109.pdf.

Shulman, L. 2007. Counting and Recounting: Assessment and the Quest for Accountability. *Change: The Magazine of Higher Learning* 39 (1): 20–25.

Sisk-Hilton, S. 2009. *Teaching and Learning in Public: Professional Development Through Shared Inquiry.* New York: Teachers College Press.

Solomon, D., D. Battistich, M. Watson, E. Schaps, and C. Lewis. 2000. "A Six-District Study of Educational Change: Direct and Mediated Effects of the Child Development Project." *Social Psychology of Education* 4: 3–51.

Stepanek, J. 2001. "A New View of Professional Development." *Northwest Teacher* 2 (2): 2–5.

Stigler, J., and J. Hiebert. 1999. *The Teaching Gap.* New York: Free Press.

Takahashi, A. 2001. Kenkyuu juygou wo dou norikiru ka (How to navigate a research lesson). In Shin Sansuu Kyouiku Kenkyuukai (New Mathematics Education Research Group) (Ed.), *Jugyou kenkyu no susumekata, fukumekata, norikirikata (How to encourage, deepen, and navigate lesson study).* Tokyo: Tooyoukan Publishing Company, 58, translation by Etsuko Tobari.

———. 2008. "Beyond Show and Tell: Neriage for Teaching Through Problem Solving." Paper presented by at the 11th International Congress on Mathematics Education, Mexico, July 8–12.

Waterman, S. 2011. Silicon Valley Mathematics Initiative: A Study of Lesson Study's Impact on Student Achievement. Retrieved February 14, 2011 from www.sumimac.org/lessonstudy.html.

Yokosuka, K. 1996. *Juugyou Kenkyuu Yougou Jiten* (Dictionary of Lesson Study Terms). Tokyo: Kyoiku Shuppan Kabushiki Kaisha.

Yoshida, M. 1999. "Lesson Study: A Case Study of a Japanese Approach to Improving Instruction Through School-Based Teacher Development." Doctoral dissertation, University of Chicago.

———. 2001. "American Educators' Interest and Hopes for Lesson Study (Jugyokenkyu) in the U.S. and What It Means for Teachers in Japan." *Journal of Japan Society of Mathematical Education* 83 (4): 24–34.